Praise for *Raise Capital on Your Own Terms*

"This is a crucial, powerful resource for businesses that need money to make their dreams come true. There are so many investors out there who are looking to move money off Wall Street and into their community. Jenny shows you how to connect with them so you can build a better world together!"

—Kate Poole, Founding Member and Leader, Regenerative Finance

"An insightful, practical, enriching book for entrepreneurs and organizations looking to build their businesses without venture capitalists. A much-needed alternative voice for entrepreneurs!"

—Aner Ben-Ami, Managing Director, Candide Group

"*Raise Capital on Your Own Terms* is a perfect motto that speaks directly to entrepreneurs. We have all that we need to create a better business funding system, and Jenny lays out the path forward."

—Vicki Saunders, founder of SheEO

"Jenny Kassan's new book turns the way entrepreneurs should look for capital upside down. It is a book for any entrepreneur, but especially mission-driven ones."

—Alicia Robb, PhD, founder and CEO, Next Wave, and Managing Partner, Next Wave Impact Fund

"Jenny Kassan is an expert on raising capital from friends, customers, and community and a leader at creating terms of investment that work for everyone."

—Morgan Simon, author of *Real Impact*

"Jenny Kassan is the go-to small business advisor. With this book, she shares her proven strategy for helping businesses raise capital on their own terms, in alignment with their values, by guiding them to finding like-minded, supportive investors."

—Kristin B. Hull, PhD, Director, Nia Community Fund

"Jenny Kassan's book is both inspirational and practical. It is inspirational because it lifts the shroud of mystery over raising capital, and it is practical because she walks the reader through the process in well-written, bite-sized chunks. This is a must-read for those new to raising capital as well as many who may think they are 'old hands'!"

—Vince Siciliano, CEO, New Resource Bank

"This should be the Bible for entrepreneurs building a small business. It makes the daunting task of raising capital easy to navigate through clear and detailed advice and innovative legal options and ownership models. These proven strategies from a national expert can empower everyone with a business plan while helping evolve capitalism into something more conscious and regenerative."
—**Michael Kramer, Managing Partner, Natural Investments, and coauthor of *The Resilient Investor***

"A major problem plagues the entrepreneurial sphere. Many of the best businesses don't reach their potential because they've not been empowered with information about how to raise capital in a way aligned with their own vision and goals. This book is a solution to that problem. It's an invaluable and groundbreaking resource that I would recommend to all entrepreneurs to expand their thinking and develop their unique right approach to raising capital. We have needed this book for a very long time, and now it is here."
—**Tara Mohr, author of *Playing Big***

"The process of raising money often dehumanizes both sides. Jenny Kassan outlines a path that allows business owners to retain their integrity and raise capital on their own terms and investors to support the real value created by business owners. A more local, more grounded, more connected kind of economy is what the legal techniques described in this book guide us toward. This is the kind of world I want to work for. I am glad to be in her orbit."
—**Kevin Jones, cofounder of Socap, Good Capital, and Neighborhood Economics**

"Jenny Kassan fulfills a desperate need for entrepreneurs seeking capital. Her book addresses the emotional, psychological, and practical barriers to seeking funds in an interconnected and easy-to-understand way. I can't recommend this book enough."
—**Nikki Silvestri, founder and CEO, Soil and Shadow**

"I'm so excited about this book! Jenny Kassan has been at the forefront of community capital, and readers could not find a better coach, mentor, and guide to this innovative way of raising capital. Prepare to have your old notions of how to raise capital turned upside down!"
—**Amy Cortese, author of *Locavesting***

raise capital
on your
own terms

HOW TO FUND YOUR BUSINESS
WITHOUT SELLING YOUR SOUL

Jenny Kassan

Foreword by Congressman Ro Khanna

Berrett–Koehler Publishers, Inc.
a BK Business book

Berrett-Koehler Publishers, Inc.
1333 Broadway, Suite 1000
Oakland, CA 94612–1921
Tel: (510) 817-2277   Fax: (510) 817-2278   www.bkconnection.com

Ordering Information
Quantity sales. Special discounts are available on quantity purchases by corporations, associations, and others. For details, contact the "Special Sales Department" at the Berrett-Koehler address above.
Individual sales. Berrett-Koehler publications are available through most bookstores. They can also be ordered directly from Berrett-Koehler: Tel: (800) 929-2929; Fax: (802) 864-7626; www.bkconnection.com
Orders for college textbook/course adoption use. Please contact Berrett-Koehler:
Tel: (800) 929-2929; Fax: (802) 864-7626.
Orders by U.S. trade bookstores and wholesalers. Please contact Ingram Publisher Services, Tel: (800) 509-4887; Fax: (800) 838-1149; E-mail: customer.service@ingrampublisherservices.com; or visit www.ingrampublisherservices.com/Ordering for details about electronic ordering.

Berrett-Koehler and the BK logo are registered trademarks of Berrett-Koehler Publishers, Inc.

Printed in the United States of America

Berrett-Koehler books are printed on long-lasting acid-free paper. When it is available, we choose paper that has been manufactured by environmentally responsible processes. These may include using trees grown in sustainable forests, incorporating recycled paper, minimizing chlorine in bleaching, or recycling the energy produced at the paper mill.

Library of Congress Cataloging-in-Publication Data

Names: Kassan, Jenny, author.
Title: Raise capital on your own terms : how to fund your business without selling your soul /
   Jenny Kassan ; foreword by Congressman Ro Khanna.
Description: First edition. | Oakland : Berrett-Koehler Publishers, 2017. |
   Includes index.
Identifiers: LCCN 2017019305 | ISBN 9781523084715 (pbk.)
Subjects: LCSH: New business enterprises—Finance. | Venture capital. | Entrepreneurship.
Classification: LCC HG4027.6 .K37 2017 | DDC 658.15/224—dc23
LC record available at https://lccn.loc.gov/2017019305

FIRST EDITION
21 20 19 18 17   10 9 8 7 6 5 4 3 2 1

Production manager: Susan Geraghty
Cover design: Irene Morris
Author photo: Jennifer Graham Photography
Interior design: Paula Goldstein
Copyeditor: Michele Jones
Composition: Westchester Publishing Services
Proofreader: Sophia Ho
Indexer: Sylvia Coates

A NOTE TO READERS

Legal disclaimer: This book serves as a guide and resource, but is not legal advice. Qualified professional counsel should be consulted for questions on your specific situation.

For readers located outside the United States of America and those seeking investment from outside the United States of America: The author is an attorney with knowledge of the law of the United States. The US laws are designed to protect US-based investors. Companies based in other countries or companies raising money from outside the United States are likely to be subject to non-US laws and should seek counsel from an attorney with knowledge of the laws of the country in which they are based and/or the countries from which they are seeking investment.

Keeping up with changes in the law: The world of raising capital, including the law that governs it, changes from time to time. For readers of this book, we have created a website with additional resources and updates: jennykassan.com /bookresources. For details on the website and other resources, see the resources section at the end of this book.

CONTENTS

A Note to Readers   vii
Foreword   xi
Introduction: You Can Raise Capital on Your Own Terms   1

PART ONE
setting the stage

Chapter 1   Busting the Myths: Forget Everything
            You Think You Know   13
Chapter 2   Are You Ready?   20
Chapter 3   The Legal Framework: What Your Lawyer
            Probably Won't Tell You   25

PART TWO
create your customized capital raising plan

Step 1   Get Clear on Your Goals and Values   33
Step 2   Identify the Right Investors for You   51
Step 3   Design Your Offer   63
Step 4   Choose Your Legal Compliance Strategy   117
Step 5   Enroll Investors   148
Step 6   Address Obstacles Head On   175

contents

Conclusion: Pulling It All Together—Your Go-to-
   Market Plan   187
Notes   193
Glossary   197
Readers' Resources Website   199
Assessments   201
   Are You Ready to Raise Capital?   201
   Capital Raising Decision Tool   203
Index   219
About the Author   231

FOREWORD

I couldn't agree more with the first sentence of this book: entrepreneurs are heroes.

Although big businesses advocate for their interests with powerful PACs and armies of corporate tax attorneys, small businesses often struggle just to survive. Yet in spite of all of the challenges they face, they have always been the backbone of our country's economy.

Small businesses represent 99.7 percent of all employer firms and employ more than half of private sector employees. Sixty-four percent of new jobs were generated by small businesses over the past fifteen years.

For our economy to thrive today, it is crucial that entrepreneurs continue taking risks to start new companies.

Since the recession, less credit has been available to small businesses. To boost our nation's economy, we need to make it easier for entrepreneurs to access capital so that they can build their businesses and hire more employees.

Trillions of dollars are invested by Americans, but almost none of that investment goes to small business. This book gives entrepreneurs the information they need to access capital from a larger number of smaller investors, opening up vast untapped resources and democratizing investing. It is a one-of-a-kind resource for entrepreneurs who want to bring in investment capital on their own terms—no matter whether nonprofit or for-profit, early stage or seasoned, on the coast or in the heartland.

In 2012, the federal government increased the legal options to facilitate investment crowdfunding. Jenny Kassan is one of the nation's leading experts on the law governing these creative tools.

The widespread use of the strategies presented in this book will unleash a new wave of entrepreneurism across America.

This book is a must-read for entrepreneurs in need of more resources and for any American who wants to invest in the vibrant small business sector of our economy.

Congressman Ro Khanna

INTRODUCTION:
YOU CAN RAISE CAPITAL
ON YOUR OWN TERMS

Entrepreneurs are heroes.

You have a dream to make a difference in the world with your product or service and make money doing it. Lots of people have dreams like that. But you are bold enough to do what it takes to turn that dream into reality.

Being an entrepreneur is not easy, but every year, hundreds of thousands of men and women in the United States decide to take a risk and start a new business.

We small business owners quickly realize that outside funding is necessary, or at least highly desirable, for our businesses to get off the ground, operate until they break even, and grow to their ideal size.

Many of us turn to our personal resources and assets as a source of business funding. We may use personal credit cards, get loans from family members, take out second and third mortgages, drive Uber, or list our spare rooms on Airbnb. We also operate on a very tight budget. We buy low-quality equipment, try to build our own websites, forgo a salary, put a moratorium on family dinners out, and generally tighten our belts for the sake of our businesses.

What we entrepreneurs need is funding that does not require sacrificing our personal credit rating, our health, our energy, or our well-being.

1

WHAT ARE THE RISKS OF RAISING FUNDING?

Unfortunately, we may shy away from seeking outside funding because of the stories we hear about the risks of bringing on outside investors.

The story of Ben & Jerry's Homemade Ice Cream is a cautionary tale of how raising funding can take your business in a direction you never intended. There are numerous such stories of mission-driven, idealistic founders losing control of their companies, only to see them begin to shed many of the things that made them great in the first place. It's stories like these that make many entrepreneurs hesitant to raise money.

Ben Cohen and Jerry Greenfield opened their first ice cream shop in Burlington, Vermont, in 1978. From the beginning, they cared about more than just profit. Ben & Jerry's "measured its own success by asking: 'How much have we improved the quality of life in the community? And how much profit is left over at the end of each month. If we haven't contributed to both those objectives, we have failed.'... For its 'Chocolate Fudge Brownie' ice cream, Ben & Jerry's purchased brownies from Greyston Bakery, an entity whose 'mission is to provide employment and support services to former homeless, low-income and disenfranchised people and their families.'"[1]

In 1984, they offered stock to Vermont residents—about eighteen hundred households became shareholders—and soon after, they took the company public.[2]

As the market for premium ice cream got more crowded, the company began to face challenges. "In 1994, the company's annual report disclosed that sales growth slowed and it had suffered its first financial loss. By 1999 the stock had dropped nearly 50 percent from its peak, because of the company's weaker financial performance."[3] This attracted interest from corporate buyers who believed they could turn things around by focusing more on the bottom line and less on the mission. *The Economist* opined that "even caring shareholders would rather that Ben & Jerry's gave its profits to charity than becoming a charity itself."[4]

When Unilever, a global corporation that owns brands ranging from Vaseline and Dove soap to Breyer's and Lipton, made an offer to buy the company at well above the current share price, the board felt that it had no choice but to accept, fearing lawsuits from disgruntled shareholders.[5] "Ben walked away from the deal with $41 million. Jerry got $9.5 million. . . . Yet Ben and Jerry have also said that losing control of their company was one of the worst experiences of their lives, and they still don't want to talk about it."[6]

The good news is that this can be avoided. You can raise capital on your own terms and not be subject to the whims of investors who care only about maximizing profits at any cost.

THE RIGHT FUNDING—WHERE DO YOU FIND IT?

You may have heard about Ben & Jerry's and other horror stories of company founders losing control of their businesses after raising money. But you need funding! You need funding that allows you to pay yourself a reasonable salary, that allows you to hire the help you need so that you can use your genius where it will contribute the most, that gives you the space to take good care of yourself so that you don't burn out and feel like giving up.

So you decide to explore the options. Maybe you Google something like "small business funding." The first links in the search results are advertisements for online lending sites that charge outrageously high interest and fees. These should only be used as a last resort when you absolutely must have an infusion of cash immediately. If you plan ahead, you should never have to turn to this incredibly expensive source of funding.

Then you see something about small business loans. You may talk to a few banks and find that you don't qualify because you don't have collateral or you haven't been in business long enough. According to a recent study, only 38 percent of businesses with revenues less than $5 million qualify for a bank loan.[7]

What about crowdfunding? You consider a Kickstarter campaign, but you worry that so many people are doing them these days that you will get lost in all the noise. And the amounts are pretty small. The majority of successful donation-based crowdfunding campaigns raise less than $10,000.[8]

What you need are investors!

When you hear the word "investor," what do you picture?

When I ask this question, most people describe a man in a suit (or, if in Silicon Valley, maybe khakis and a button-down shirt) in a fancy office spending every workday combing through pitch decks, executive summaries, and due diligence, and barking tough questions at terrified entrepreneurs. These are the kinds of investors who will not allow you to raise capital on your own terms. These kinds of investors expect you to accept *their* terms, take them or leave them.

I call these folks *professional investors*. These are wealthy individuals and organizations, sometimes investing their own money and sometimes investing on behalf of others. They come in many flavors: angel investors, venture capitalists, private equity funds, family offices, private foundations, wealth managers, and so on. These are the kinds of investors who pushed Ben & Jerry's to sell to the highest bidder. (Of course, not all professional investors put financial return ahead of all other considerations. There is a growing movement called **impact investing,** which considers community and environmental impact as well as financial returns when making investment decisions.)

When entrepreneurs think that professional investors are the only source of investment, many of them quickly dismiss the idea of raising capital.

I hear them say things like this:

+ Why would these people even consider investing in my business? I doubt I could give them what they're looking for.
+ I wouldn't know how to get my foot in the door with these people or even how to find them.
+ Don't these investors want to take control of the businesses they invest in? Don't they even sometimes fire the founder? I'm not ready to give up control.
+ How could I stay true to my company's mission and values if I had to focus all my efforts on giving my investors the highest possible financial returns at any cost?

If you limit yourself to seeking funding from professional investors, you may be right to have fears and concerns. As we'll discuss in greater detail, these kinds of investors tend to follow a very specific investment model that is not a good fit for most businesses and may well not be a good fit for you.

The good news is that there are many sources of investment capital, and even if professional investors aren't right for you, I can almost guarantee that there are investors out there who *are* right for you. We will talk a lot more in later chapters about all the options, but for now, just know that businesses of all kinds can raise money from investors. Just because you don't have the type of business that would be attractive to professional investors or you're unwilling to accept the strings that come with their investments does not mean that you cannot raise hundreds of thousands and even millions of dollars from investors. There are investors who will be happy to support you *on your own terms* and not push you to sacrifice your goals and values.

HOW TO TAP THE MOST ABUNDANT YET OVERLOOKED SOURCE OF BUSINESS FUNDING

This book takes you through a step-by-step process to design a capital raising plan to tap the right investors for you. Statistically speaking, these investors are likely not professionals. They are far more likely to be regular folks with day jobs that do not involve investing. These people are by far the most abundant source of investment capital, yet very few business owners consider tapping them.

There are six basic steps to creating a capital raising plan that is customized to your particular situation. You *must* design a capital raising plan that fits who you are, your goals, and your values. Using a one-size-fits-all approach to bringing on investors is one of the surest ways to make your life a living hell. It is critical to create as much alignment as possible between what you want and what your investors want. Don't rush into raising money. Use this book to create a plan that will result in more peace, joy, and prosperity in your business and life.

Never trust anyone who tells you there is only one way to raise capital. There are infinite ways, and there is at least one that is right for you. This book takes you through a step-by-step process to design your plan—the one that inspires you, excites you, and is in complete alignment with your goals and values.

These steps are not linear—creating your capital raising plan is an iterative process. For example, what you discover when working through step 2 may lead you to return to step 1 and make refinements. Each decision you make will help you refine your other decisions, so don't hesitate to revisit steps until you feel that your plan is doable and that it truly reflects your uniqueness.

The following is a summary of the steps that we will cover in detail in this book.

Step 1: Get Clear on Your Goals and Values

Your goals and values are the foundation for your capital raising plan. To some, this may seem obvious, but it amazes me how many entrepreneurs attempt to find investors without any thought to whether their potential investors' goals and values are in alignment with their own.

Which of the following statements apply to you?

+ I don't want to give up any control—I want to make the important decisions in my business.
+ I know my business has the potential to grab market share, so I want to grow as fast as possible and beat the competition.
+ I want to make my business attractive for sale to a larger company in the next five to seven years; any buyer is fine as long as I can walk away with a big check.
+ I would be open to considering the sale of my business, but I don't want to be pressured to sell it to a buyer who won't continue to uphold the high standards associated with my brand.
+ I want my business to grow to X size and then stay pretty steady from there; I just want my business to provide a reliable source of income and remain a manageable size.
+ I would like to keep my business in my family for generations.
+ Someday, I would like to convert my business into a co-op or other kind of stakeholder-owned business so that the workers, producers, and/or customers can take over the ownership and control.

Whichever of these goals, or others, resonate with you will have a big effect on what kinds of investors you target and the offering you make to them. In part 2, step 1, I'll tell you exactly how your goals and values will inform your capital raising plan.

Step 2: Identify the Right Investors for You

Investors are incredibly diverse. More than 50 percent of the adult population of the United States is an investor. There are millions of potential investors out there, and you need only a few.

Once you understand all of the different sources of investment and what each one is looking for, you will be able to decide where to focus your efforts.

Getting as much clarity as possible on the characteristics of your ideal investors will help you home in on the right ones and avoid wasting time on the wrong ones.

This is what we cover in part 2, step 2.

Step 3: Design Your Offer

There is a literally infinite number of investment types that you can offer to investors. The basic categories include equity, straight debt, revenue-based debt, convertible debt, and agreements for future equity.

Within each of these, there are numerous provisions that can be customized to your particular situation. For example,

+ Do your investors have voting rights, and if so, what are they specifically?
+ Do you regularly share profits with your investors, and if so, how much and when?
+ How will you and your investors be taxed?

♦ How will your investors exit from their investment (i.e., get their original investment back)?

♦ How should your offering be priced?

These are just a few of the choices you need to make.

In part 2, step 3, you'll design an offering that fits your goals, values, and target investors.

Step 4: Choose Your Legal Compliance Strategy

I passed the bar and worked as a lawyer for eleven years before I realized that you cannot just go out and talk to potential investors without first nailing down your compliance strategy under both state and federal law.

In the early years of the twentieth century, the states and Congress passed a lot of laws designed to protect people from making investments without knowing all the relevant facts. These laws are collectively called *securities law*. Securities law is a bit tricky, but once you understand the basics, you should be able to choose the strategy that fits you best.

The strategy you choose will affect to whom you can make your offering, who can actually invest, and how you can get the word out. Before making an offering to any potential investor, it is essential to choose your legal compliance strategy.

In part 2, step 4, I'll lay out your options and the pros and cons of each.

Step 5: Enroll Investors

Once you know what you're offering, to whom you're offering it, and how you're going to reach investors, it's time to work on your enrollment skills. There is no one-size-fits-all way to communicate with investors. Your enrollment strategy will depend on who your target investors are.

In part 2, step 5, I'll help you tailor your enrollment strategy to the investors you're targeting. This includes getting meetings, what to say in meetings, and what materials to share.

Step 6: Address Obstacles Head On

This step is one that many entrepreneurs skip, but I have come to believe that it is perhaps the most important of all. This step involves working on the mental game of preparing for and staying on track during your capital raising journey. No matter how amazing your business and how great your offering, unaddressed mind-set obstacles can make raising money almost impossible.

In part 2, step 6, I'll share some tools and exercises that can make the difference between a stalled fundraising effort and a joyful sprint to the finish line.

ABOUT THIS BOOK

This book teaches the steps to take to greatly increase your chances of success with raising capital on your own terms.

In part 1, we'll explore the landscape of investment capital. It is far larger and more diverse than many lawyers and business advisors would have you believe. We'll bust some myths about investors, who they are, and what they're looking for. We'll explore how ready you are to raise capital. We'll also begin to discuss the law governing capital raising because without having a basic understanding of that set of laws and regulations, you will always be at the mercy of lawyers who may not know what they're talking about. For better or worse, raising capital is a highly regulated activity. The good news is that if you are armed with the knowledge of how these laws work, you can get very creative in how you raise money.

In part 2, I'll take you through the step-by-step process summarized in the previous section to create a capital raising plan that is tailored to your unique situation. One of the biggest mistakes entrepreneurs make when raising capital is to simply launch into talking to investors without a clear plan. This leads to a lot of wasted time—if you're lucky. If you're not so lucky, you could inadvertently break the law and find yourself with investors who are not a good fit and can make your life miserable.

Once you've worked through part 2, you will have a clear vision for how to find the capital you need from the perfect investors for you.

In the conclusion, we'll pull it all together so that you can actually go out and raise the money.

I have included a glossary at the end to provide more detailed definitions of some of the capital raising terms used throughout the book. Terms that are defined in the glossary are boldfaced in the text.

I recommend that you have a notebook or journal dedicated to designing and implementing your capital raising strategy. As you go through the book, keep your notes, decisions, and insights in your journal.

busting the myths

FORGET EVERYTHING YOU THINK YOU KNOW

The amount of misinformation and confusion out there about raising capital from investors is staggering! I cannot tell you how many times I have been at presentations by "experts" and listened with amazement as they confidently informed the audience of "facts" about capital raising that were completely incorrect. If experts like lawyers and finance specialists are so often wrong on this topic, imagine how hard it is for the layperson entrepreneur to get the full and correct picture.

I have been on a mission for years to rectify this situation, which is why I wrote this book. Because so many lawyers and other so-called experts seem to be too lazy to take the time to understand the full spectrum of capital raising options and because they also seem to be unwilling to admit when they don't actually know something, entrepreneurs are constantly making huge mistakes with their capital raising efforts that can cost them time, money, and even their business.

Why am I so well qualified to give you the truth about capital raising? Due to an accident of my career path, my approach to capital raising is different from that of most lawyers.

I started my legal career as in-house counsel at a non-profit organization in Oakland, California. While I was there, I worked on lots of very interesting projects, such as building a mixed-use transit-oriented real estate development and starting and running businesses that were subsidiaries of the nonprofit, with the goal of creating jobs and wealth in the low-income community where the nonprofit was based. After eleven years, I left to join a small boutique law firm that focused on helping mission-driven businesses (aka *social enterprises*—any business that makes a positive impact in the world through its products or services, its contribution to its community, its treatment of its workers and suppliers, and/or its commitment to caring for the environment) start up and raise capital. The founder of the law firm was one of the nation's top securities lawyers. I barely knew what securities law was! He taught me that securities law is what governs how businesses can raise money from investors. I started to learn about securities law, and found it fascinating. So, even though I had eleven years of experience as a lawyer, I approached this area of law with a beginner's mind. I had never learned all the conventional wisdom about how securities law is practiced. (Luckily, the founder of the firm was very open minded and entrepreneurial, so he didn't fill my head with the conventional wisdom either.) Though I didn't know it at the time, I was approaching securities law in the way described by Dorie Clark in this quotation from her book *Stand Out*:

> Every field has useful guiding assumptions. Received
> wisdom saves time—you don't have to reinvent the
> wheel . . . but it can also be a trap, preventing you from
> exploring new ideas . . . You don't succeed by following
> the rules and thinking exactly like everyone else; you
> need to ask "what if?" and "why not?" . . . What would
> [an outsider] make of how things are typically done? . . .
> Might there be a new or different way of doing things?[9]

This attitude allowed me to see possibilities that other securities lawyers didn't seem even to be aware of.

Most lawyers try several different practice areas and find that there is one area of law that they really enjoy. For me, that was securities law. There was something about it that I found fascinating, fun, and exciting. I was completely hooked on learning as much about it as I could. I read every book I could get my hands on, talked to every securities lawyer I could pin down, and read the actual statutes, rules, and case law. Believe it or not, a lot of lawyers never bother to do this. It is amazing all the things you can find when you really read this stuff. I'll give you a nerdy example of this: There was a young aspiring lawyer who was apprenticing for me. I asked her to look something up in the California securities statute. She said, "Jenny, have you ever noticed Section 25102(e) of the statute? It is a provision that exempts privately offered debt from the usual compliance requirements!" We were both really excited to discover this little nugget in the law that would make it a lot easier for some of our clients to raise capital.

I spent years studying the law of capital raising. I assumed that all securities lawyers knew the same things I did, but I found out that many of them don't. This is because there is a certain well-worn pathway for raising capital that is relatively easy for lawyers to follow for their clients. This is the pathway used by businesses that are raising money from professional investors like angels and venture capitalists. Most lawyers don't bother to learn any other pathway. This is a real shame, because there are many others. I love to help entrepreneurs figure out the exact right one for them.

So forget everything you think you know about raising capital from investors. I promise you that this book contains legally correct information and contains basically *all* of the legally correct information about how small businesses can raise money from investors—not just the truth, but the whole truth. Of course, as I noted earlier, the law does change from time to time, so please check the readers' resources website for updates. (See the resources section at the end of the book for details on how to access it.)

LET'S BUST SOME MYTHS

Let's bust some myths about what it means to raise money from investors. Here is some of the conventional wisdom that you've probably heard or read on the Internet:

1. You can only raise money from investors if you are going to grow your business very fast and have a "liquidity event" (sale of the company or initial public offering [IPO]) in which the investors make thirty to fifty times their initial investment.

2. Try to delay offering equity to investors for as long as you can because that is the most expensive money you can get.
3. Even though you have to give up a lot of ownership and control when you raise money, the good thing about it is that your investors have experience and contacts in your industry, so they can advise you and make great connections for you.
4. The investors set the terms of the investment—you are at their mercy.
5. If you raise money from investors, you have to give up control, and your investors become your boss.
6. Once you have investors, you must put their interests first, above those of all other stakeholders, or you risk being sued.
7. Investors consist of very wealthy individuals and organizations. They are all looking for basically the same thing, and you need to tailor your business to fit what they are looking for.

Although these statements are true for certain types of investors and investments, they are not universally true. In fact, in my experience (having helped my clients raise millions of dollars and having raised several hundred thousand for my own business), the following statements are true:

1. The vast majority of investors are satisfied with a financial return that is much less ambitious than what angels and venture capitalists demand. (Note that studies of the venture capital industry demonstrate that actual returns are much lower than the hype would suggest.)

And most investors consider a lot more than financial return when making investment decisions.

2. You can design any type of investment offering you want—it does not have to be "expensive."

3. It is possible to raise capital (equity or debt) without giving up any control.

4. Investors can get healthy returns from steady-state businesses (i.e., ones that do not grow explosively). A liquidity event is not required for investors to get paid back.

5. The "smart money" that supposedly comes from professional investors (i.e., all that expertise that we are told they have) is questionable. Some professional investors can be a huge asset to the companies they invest in; others will take the company in the completely wrong direction. The founders often know a lot more about the right direction to take their business than an outside investor does.

6. It is possible to design a company and its financing strategy in a way that reduces the likelihood of lawsuits for failure to maximize investor return.

7. The universe of investors encompasses far more than angels and venture capitalists, and each investor is unique.

Let me quote one investor I know, Kate Poole, so you can really get a sense of how truly opposite of the stereotypical investor a real investor can be:

> I lived at an anti-capitalist commune in Thailand and
> got really fired up about how capitalism was destroying

people and the planet. I wanted to do something to fight capitalism. I found out that my family's wealth was invested in huge evil mega-corporations that were destroying the planet and communities and extracting wealth in an unhealthy way. I organize other young people with wealth to shift control of capital to communities that are most affected by economic and climate crises, especially racialized wealth extraction. As a white inheritor of wealth, I want to invest back in the communities wealth has been taken from.[10]

I hope that you are starting to believe that raising capital from investors can be very different from the much-hyped venture capital model celebrated on the cover of *Fast Company* magazine.

In the next chapter, we will dive into determining how ready you are to raise capital.

are you ready?

You may have been **bootstrapping** for a while now—using your personal resources to fund your business and hoping that eventually you will be able to break even and start paying yourself and buying the things your business needs out of revenues.

You probably picked up this book because you are getting tired of bootstrapping. You're tired of working long hours because you can't afford a web designer or bookkeeper, forgoing a salary, and monitoring every penny your family spends. You're tired of not being able to give the best possible service to your customers because you can't afford the highest-quality equipment and suppliers or because you're so busy dealing with administrative issues that you don't have time to stay on top of new developments in your field.

You're quickly coming to the realization that an under-resourced business is a nightmare for the business owner and her customers alike.

Now don't get me wrong. I know that almost every entrepreneur needs to make sacrifices during the start-up phase. But there must be an end in sight. If you go on too long with a business that is keeping you overworked, over-whelmed, and broke, you will burn out and fall out of love with the entrepreneurial journey. And your customers may get tired of dealing with an exhausted, burned-out service provider who is trying to wear all the hats in her business.

Going for too long with too few resources is a leading cause of business failure. And you may get so tired of living like this that you decide to give up and look for a job.

This would be a real shame, because the world needs as many people as possible to turn their big, bold difference-making visions into reality.

> *Don't ask yourself what the world needs. Ask yourself what makes you come alive and then go do that. Because what the world needs is people who have come alive.*
> —HOWARD THURMAN

You owe it to yourself, your family, and all the lives you have the potential to touch with your business to figure out how to get the resources you need for your business to thrive. And the sooner you start, the better. Finding the right funding for you can take many months. Start now so that you get the resources you need long before you start to feel desperate. Raising money when you're desperate is one of the hardest things an entrepreneur has to do. Congratulations—you have taken the first step by picking up this book.

How do you know whether you're ready? Turn to Are You Ready to Raise Capital in the assessments section at the back of the book to help you determine how ready you are and what you may need to do to get ready. The more questions you can answer with an emphatic yes, the more ready you are to raise money from investors.

For each of the questions in the assessment, make sure to write detailed notes about the answers in your journal. For example, saying you know who your competitors are and what makes you different from them is a lot less powerful than making a list of your competitors and writing down how you differentiate yourself from each one.

If you are limiting your business's impact and growth potential because you don't think that you're ready to raise capital, you are selling yourself short and denying yourself a huge opportunity, not to mention depriving the world of the impact you could have if you achieve your business's full potential.

Right now, you may be saying to yourself, *Do you seriously believe that* any *business that can answer yes to most of those questions can raise money from investors? That can't possibly be true!*

You're absolutely right. I do not believe that any business can raise money. To put a finer point on it, I do not believe that any business can raise money at any point in time. A business that is ready to raise money now may not have been ready one year ago. But I do believe that any business that isn't ready can get ready. So I take it back: maybe I *do* believe that any business can raise money from investors!

NOW WHAT?

Maybe you answered yes to quite a few of the questions in the assessment, but you're still having doubts about whether you can successfully raise money from investors.

In this book, I will share examples from real life entrepreneurs I've worked with who (to the untrained eye) looked like extremely unlikely candidates for bringing on investors and reaching their capital raising goals. I'll admit that even I have been surprised when some of my clients reached their goals! But I have been amazed time after time as I've seen so many entrepreneurs of incredibly diverse backgrounds, geographies, and industries use the steps that I am going to share with you in this book to raise the money they needed from investors who were incredibly supportive.

On the basis of my ten years of experience helping entrepreneurs raise money, I honestly believe that if you follow the steps in this book, you will reach your capital raising goal. Will it be easy? Probably not, although it may be. Many of my clients have approached the capital raising process as though they were throwing a big party. So much of what the experience is like for you will depend on how you approach it and your beliefs about it. If you approach it with the belief that it will be really hard, it probably will be. If you approach it with the belief that it will be a fun and exciting process, it is more likely to be that!

All I ask right now is that you put your skepticism aside, as well as anything you may have read or heard about raising capital, and approach the capital raising journey as you would anything else in your business: as a challenge to be greeted with ingenuity and a sense of adventure and without assumptions that limit your creativity.

It is natural to be nervous and maybe even terrified at the prospect of raising capital. Every entrepreneur experiences those fears and doubts. The key is to (1) know the options, (2) choose an option that fits your situation, and (3) feel the fear and do it anyway. As you move forward step-by-step, your confidence will grow.

Raising capital has many benefits beyond the obvious one of having more money.

I believe that raising capital is a major growth experience. When you finish, you will not be the same person you were when you started.

You will be stronger, more resourceful, and better able to see the value of what you are building as an entrepreneur. You will take on more leadership roles and take bigger leaps toward fulfilling your dreams for both your business and every other part of your life. You will be less likely to settle for things that are not working for you.

If you, like so many entrepreneurs I know, have always had trouble really believing in the value of what you offer, the process of raising capital will help you confront this limitation and grow your confidence.

Beyond that, if you follow the steps in this book, your investors will become a tribe of committed supporters whom you can call on in good and bad times.

Raising capital for your business provides greater tangible and intangible benefits than almost anything else you can do as an entrepreneur. It is an endeavor worthy of some serious attention, time, and energy. So let's dig in!

CHAPTER 3

the legal framework

WHAT YOUR LAWYER PROBABLY WON'T TELL YOU

To understand the law governing capital raising, it's helpful to understand the history of these laws, known collectively as securities law.

The securities laws were adopted early in the twentieth century to protect regular folks from slick pitch artists who traveled across the country selling worthless investments. Kansas adopted the first securities law in 1911 to "keep 'Kansas money in Kansas' and help local farmers and small businesses rather than enriching 'New York Stock Exchange speculators and gamblers.'"[11]

Other states followed suit, and eventually the federal government adopted its own securities laws starting in 1933.

The primary purpose of these laws is to protect the public from investing without first receiving full disclosure of exactly what they may be getting into. To that end, offerings of securities are required to be "registered" before any offer or sale can take place. A registration involves the filing of extensive disclosure materials with the relevant regulatory authorities. The securities regulators then review the disclosures; when the regulators are satisfied that the disclosures are sufficient to protect the investing public, they give the go-ahead to begin offering the securities. There are some significant exceptions to this registration requirement, which we will cover in great detail a bit later.

WHAT IS A SECURITY?

The first question to ask when you want to raise money for your business is whether you are offering a security. If what you are offering falls within the definition of a security, then you need to make sure you are complying with applicable securities law. If what you are offering is not a security, there is no need to worry about the securities laws.

For example, let's say you decide to raise money on a crowdfunding website like Indiegogo or Kickstarter. In exchange for contributions from your backers, you offer them recognition on your website. This fundraising strategy does not involve an offering of securities, so you don't have to worry about securities compliance.

So, what *is* a security?

Generally, it is any arrangement that allows the contributor of funds to receive a financial return on his or her investment. Recognition on your website would not be considered a return on investment. But if you offer the contributor $110 in one year in exchange for $100 now, the investor is receiving a financial return of $10 on her investment. That would be a security, and you would need to make sure your offering complies with securities law.

The most common types of securities are stock (ownership shares in a corporation), limited liability company memberships (ownership interests in an LLC), and promissory notes (the document that you use when you borrow money from someone). Some people think that a loan is not a security and that only an equity investment is a security. That is not the case! Any investment instrument that pays a financial return to someone who is not actively involved in management is a security, regardless of whether the return consists of profit sharing, interest, appreciation in value, or anything else. In part 2, step 3, we will discuss all of the different kinds of securities you can offer—the possibilities are infinite!

You may think that it's best to try to raise money in a way that allows you to avoid compliance with the securities laws. Wanting to avoid securities compliance is one reason why so many people raise money on donation-based crowdfunding websites. But I believe that it is much easier to raise significant amounts of funding when you offer a security because a financial return on investment is generally much more attractive than what you can offer without using securities (e.g., a T-shirt or recognition on your website). Also, there are so many donation- and perks-based crowdfunding campaigns going on at any given moment that it's very hard to stand out from the crowd. Far fewer businesses raise funding by offering securities to investors, so it is much easier to get attention, and your costs to get the word out are likely to be much lower.

You don't have to be intimidated by the thought of offering a security. Although securities law is not the easiest thing in the world to understand, this book will explain the basics in layperson's terms and make it possible for you to offer an investment opportunity without breaking the law.

SECURITIES LAW 101

If you want to offer a security to investors, you must *first* get clear on your securities compliance strategy. If you start offering your investment opportunity without having this in place, you may inadvertently limit your options or even break the law, which can create potential liabilities, such as fines and the requirement to return all of your investors' money.

You know how there are some areas of life that are regulated by both state and federal law? For example, if you live in Colorado, it's legal under Colorado law to use marijuana, but the very same activity is illegal under federal law. Well, it is kind of the same thing with securities law. Generally speaking, you need to create a securities compliance plan for both federal law *and* for the laws of any states where you want to offer your investment opportunity. So let's say you have a business in Montana and a list of potential investors who live in Montana and South Dakota. This means that you have to figure out a compliance plan for federal securities law as well as for the securities laws of both Montana and South Dakota.

The general rule is that before you make an offering of securities, you must register the offering with the relevant authorities. For the federal government, this is the Securities and Exchange Commission (SEC). For the states, it is whatever branch of government regulates **securities offerings** in that state. The process of registering your offering with the SEC is extremely time consuming and expensive. (It is the process that companies must complete when they "go public," aka do an IPO.) State registration tends to be much easier than federal. The good news is that there are several exemptions from this general registration requirement, under both federal and state law. This book will not cover the steps for completing a federal registration because for smaller businesses, there are numerous ways to raise money legally without having to do that, but we will discuss state registration. Sometimes there is an interaction between federal and state law—some federal-level compliance options preempt states' ability to impose some kinds of requirements. We will discuss this in more detail in part 2, step 4. But first, to understand your legal compliance options, you need to understand two important concepts in securities law: the accredited investor and the public versus private offering.

What Is an Accredited Investor?

An **accredited investor** is defined under federal securities law as an individual with at least $200,000 in annual income or $1 million in net worth, not including her primary residence. (This is just a partial definition—for a complete definition, see the glossary.) Accredited investors make up approximately 10 percent of the population.[12]

Securities law assumes that accredited investors are better able to protect their interests than the rest of us. Therefore, certain legal compliance strategies include requirements limiting the ability to include unaccredited investors in your offering and/or sale of securities. (You are making an *offer* when you tell someone about the opportunity to invest, and you are making a *sale* when someone actually invests; securities laws regulate both offers and sales.) Many attorneys advise their clients not to even talk to unaccredited investors. Why would an attorney advise his client to leave 90 percent of the population out of a securities offering? My guess is that many attorneys are not familiar enough with the legal compliance strategies that allow the inclusion of unaccredited investors to feel comfortable with those options. Some attorneys also believe that unaccredited investors might be more litigious than accredited investors, but I have never seen any empirical data to support this. (If anything, I would guess that the opposite is more likely to be true.)

There are many legal strategies that allow you to include both accredited and unaccredited investors (what I call the "100 percent"). If you have an attorney who will not even entertain a strategy that includes them, you may want to find a different attorney!

What Is a Public versus a Private Offering?

Securities law assumes that if you go around shouting from the rooftops that you are offering an investment opportunity, there is greater risk to the investing public. The idea is that people who don't know anything about you and your company might invest on a whim and end up losing all their money. Because of this, certain legal compliance strategies require you to keep your offering private. The distinction between a public and a private offering is not always obvious or clear, but generally, a private offering involves one-on-one conversations with potential investors, and a public offering involves advertising (e.g., social media posts, speeches at public events, and press releases).

A NOTE FOR NONPROFIT ORGANIZATIONS

Some people assume that a nonprofit can only raise money through grants and donations (i.e., money that is never returned to the contributor). However, it is completely possible for a nonprofit to raise money from investors. For example, Nia House, a nonprofit preschool in Berkeley, California, offered the opportunity for the parents of their students and other community stakeholders to invest in loans to the school. The source of repayment is the tuition charged by the school. A nonprofit that generates enough revenue to pay a financial return to investors can raise money from investors.

Nonprofits often have an easier time with the legal compliance requirements for raising capital. They are exempt from the federal registration requirements, and many states have a similar exemption. Raising capital from investors can therefore be a great option for nonprofits.

CONCLUSION

The purpose of this chapter was to give you a sense of the basic framework of securities law. We will get into specific compliance options in part 2, step 4.

The following are the main variables that will affect what legal compliance strategy you choose:

+ Do you want to be able to include both accredited and unaccredited investors, or do you want to limit your offering to accredited investors only? Also, if you want to include unaccredited investors, how many would you like to be able to have?

+ Do you want to be able to publicly advertise your securities offering?
+ In what states do you want to offer your securities? Just one? A few? All of them?
+ How much do you want to raise?

If you can answer those questions, you will be able to choose the right legal compliance strategy for you. Watch out for lawyers who prescribe a one-size-fits-all strategy! There are numerous options, and chances are there is one that will allow you to raise money in the perfect way for you.

get clear on your goals and values

Before you start to raise money, you need to get really clear on your goals and values. If you don't design your capital raising strategy with your goals and values in mind, you run the risk of raising money in a way that will require you to sacrifice what is most important to you.

Don't just take it from me. Here is some advice from Greg Steltenpohl, founder of Odwalla Inc. juice company, in a speech he gave in 2013:

> Us entrepreneurs don't think nearly enough about the decision of who you get in bed with with the money. You put some real thought into who you partner with, but when it comes time to go get the money, you just want the money, and you're so happy that someone believes in you that you take the money. It's crazy.[13]

Greg speaks from painful experience. His investors forced a sale of the company to Coca-Cola, which was completely out of alignment with the founders' goals and values. Sadly, as I mentioned earlier in this book, far too many company founders end up with investors who pressure them to do things they would rather not do, and sometimes even fire them from their own company.

How can you design your capital raising strategy from the very beginning to avoid future conflicts with your investors?

First, take some time to get as clear as possible about what's important to you about your business. This step will help you do that.

Second, make sure you understand the motivations of the different kinds of investors. There are some investors whose goals may be inherently misaligned with yours. Knowing that in advance will help you avoid wasting time on the wrong investors. We will talk more about different kinds of investors in step 2.

WHAT ARE GOALS AND VALUES?

Before jumping in to getting clear on your goals and values, I want to define exactly what I mean by these terms. There are many different pieces of this puzzle, all of which should be clear to you before you raise money.

Values include

- How you want your employees to be treated
- How you want your suppliers to be treated
- Quality standards for your product or service
- Standards related to your contractors (e.g., would you contract with a manufacturer that has been fined by the EPA for polluting?)

+ What effect you want your business to have on the environment (e.g., air quality, production of waste, carbon footprint)
+ What effect you want your business to have on the communities where it does business
+ Your view of the importance of transparency (e.g., whether you want to share detailed information about your company with your employees, investors, and maybe even the general public)

Goals include

+ How many hours per week you want to work
+ How much vacation you want to take
+ What salary you want to pay yourself
+ How big you want your company to grow
+ How quickly you want your company to grow
+ How long you want to run your company
+ What you want to have happen with your company when you're ready to leave it
+ How you want your company to affect the world
+ How much control you want over major decisions

Of course, your goals and values can change over time as your company evolves. But the clearer you are now about what is important to you, the easier it will be for you to make sure that your company continues to be in service to those goals and values.

Some entrepreneurs may want to cut to the chase and skip this part. But it is well worth the time and effort to get clear on your goals and values *before* designing your capital raising strategy. Spending time on this up front is one of the best investments you can make to avoid the heartache of seeing your business being pushed in a direction that is not right for you.

YOUR WHY

Think about why you started your business in the first place. Was it to have autonomy and freedom? Was it so that you could travel the world? Was it so that you could create jobs for people in your community? Was it to create financial security for you and your loved ones? Was it so that you could work no more than twenty hours per week?

Whatever you do, never make a decision in your business that will require you to sacrifice the whole reason you started your business in the first place. For example, if you love having free time to pursue your hobbies, don't bring on an investor who expects you to devote all your waking hours to the company. Don't be one of those entrepreneurs who wakes up one day and realizes that she hates the business she has built.

Did you start your business to have an impact in the world? For example, maybe you've created an app that will disrupt the banking industry and make high-quality financial services affordable and accessible to everyone. Your goal is probably to reach as many customers as possible as quickly as possible. And you may be wary of selling the company to a large bank that is more concerned with maximizing profit than serving low-income customers.

Or maybe you started a fresh juice bar because you want the people in your community to be healthier and you want to support local farmers. In that case, you wouldn't be concerned with reaching massive numbers of customers globally, but you would want to grow your customer base within your local community. And you probably would not want to compromise on your commitment to getting the freshest local produce even if it's not always the cheapest option.

Take some time to write down your why. Why do you want to have a business in the first place? As you raise money, revisit from time to time what you wrote and check to make sure that the decisions you're making in your business, including which potential investors you're talking to, are serving your why.

YOUR VISION

Picture what your business will look like when all your dreams about it have come true. Is it a giant multinational company listed on the New York Stock Exchange? Is it a small local business that is known for giving back to the community? Is it a business that has ten employees—or ten thousand? What impact is it having on you, your family, your employees, your suppliers, your investors, the people who live near its facilities, public policy, the environment? Are you still in control, or maybe you've given up your controlling interest in the name of scaling your impact? Are you the CEO, involved in all the major decisions, or an advisor who holds the big vision? Or something in between?

Write down in as much detail as possible what the business looks like when it has reached its ideal state. This vision serves as a road map to help you choose the best strategy for raising money.

You may find this a difficult exercise because there can be so many outside influences that affect what you think you want your business to be. There are messages coming at you from every direction about what it means to be a success—the media, your friends, your upbringing, your cultural heritage, and so on. Try as hard as you can to put those messages aside and home in on what success means to you. If you work toward someone else's idea of success, you are far less likely to meet your goals. Plus, if you do achieve this sort of "success," you may not be very happy! Spend as much time as you need to search inside and find out what really lights you up. That is the business that will make you happy and that the world needs you to build!

YOUR NONNEGOTIABLES

Picture an investor walking up to you and offering a check for $1 million. What conditions would make you refuse the check? The following are examples of issues that some investors might want you to compromise on. Be very honest with yourself about which of these are nonnegotiables for you.

- ☐ I want to keep control; I want the freedom to do what I want with my business.
- ☐ I want to pay my employees a living wage and provide good benefits.

☐ I want to source only from suppliers that are fair-trade certified.

☐ I want to contribute X percent of my gross revenues to Y charity.

☐ I do not want to work more than forty hours per week so that I can spend time with my family.

☐ I do not want to use artificial colors or flavors in my product.

☐ Other: _____

_____

_____.

I'm not recommending that you be rigid and uncompromising. But most of us have values that are so important to us that compromising on them would make it hard for us to look at ourselves in the mirror. Be sure to take the time now to write down those nonnegotiables. Doing so will make it much easier to home in on the right investors for you. There are investors who share your values and will be thrilled that you have committed not to compromise on them.

YOUR BUSINESS GOALS

Finding the right investors requires that you have an idea about where you want to take your business over the next five to ten years.

Which of the following goals are true for you?

☐ I want to grow my business as fast as possible.

☐ I want to make my business attractive for sale to a larger company in the next five to seven years.

☐ I would be open to considering the sale of my business, but I don't want to be pressured to sell it to the wrong buyer.

☐ I want my business to grow to X size and then stay pretty steady from there; I don't think growth beyond a certain point is necessarily a good thing.

☐ I would like to keep my business in my family for generations.

☐ I want to take my company public (i.e., do an IPO).

☐ I would like to convert my business into a cooperative someday so that the workers, producers, and/or customers can take over the ownership and control and I can retire.

As we will discuss in greater detail in steps 2 and 3, one of the greatest sources of misalignment between entrepreneurs and investors is the **exit strategy.** The exit strategy defines how and when the investor will get her money back out of the investment, and how much return (i.e., additional money beyond the amount of her investment) she will get in the popular media.

There is a much-hyped model of investing—I'll refer to it as the venture capital (VC) model—that is based on the assumption that the investee must grow as fast as possible with the single-minded intention that it will be acquired for a high price (aka valuation). Although very few companies actually raise capital using this model, it seems to be the only model that gets attention or is considered valid in the popular media.

The good news is that a small but growing number of professional investors are recognizing that this model should not be the only game in town. For example, Aner Ben-Ami of Pi Investments, a firm that manages investments for wealthy families, has noted that

> [Most enterprises] are very unlikely to have the growth/ scale trajectory and to generate the kind of exit that [venture capitalists are looking for]. This doesn't mean they are inferior businesses—they are simply designed for a different purpose and have a different path to success. If we try to shoehorn this diverse set of businesses into standard venture terms (as we're currently doing), we'll end up with one of two outcomes: (1) Businesses that have a very real chance of being financially viable will not get funded . . . [or] (2) Businesses get pushed to aggressively pursue a growth trajectory that may be unrealistic or counterproductive for them.[14]

Ben-Ami stated in a recent webinar that companies which receive this kind of funding are expected to push the gas pedal aggressively and to prioritize growth over profitability. This strategy increases the likelihood of failure. That is why venture capitalists expect a high percentage of their investees to fail. Although that high a failure rate is just part of doing business for the venture capitalist, for the entrepreneur, as well as her family, community, employees, and suppliers, it can be devastating.[15] According to Ben-Ami, only ten to twenty deals per year drive 90 percent of the returns in the VC industry. All of the other VC investees are basically relegated to the dustbin of history.[16]

Jonathan Nelson, the CEO of Hackers/Founders, a network of global tech founders based in Silicon Valley, says that the venture capital model considers a profitable company that has employees and is growing steadily year over year to be a failure because it is not growing fast enough. In Silicon Valley terms, these companies are known as "zombies." Jonathan spent many years in the health care industry, and he jokes that any doctor who had a success rate similar to that of venture capitalists (the industry standard is that only one in ten investees grows fast enough and has a big enough "exit" to be considered a success) would have his license suspended![17]

Blair Enns, author of *The Win without Pitching Manifesto*, has said,

> There's a large segment of the tech world that lauds the serial entrepreneur, but I'll admit I've never understood it. These people are admired for how many companies they've spun up and exited but I never hear anybody taking stock of what happens to those businesses after they get acquired. I wonder how many of these exits end up being good for both the acquirer and the customer? I also wonder what those entrepreneurs could accomplish if they focused all their superpowers on just one endeavor?[18]

Note that of the Inc. 500, an annual list of the five hundred fastest-growing private companies in the United States, only 6.5 percent raised venture funding.[19] Obviously, there are ways to build businesses that do not involve VCs!

The good news is that there are vast amounts of funding available for small business that do not use the VC model. Before pursuing VC-style investment, be certain that the model fits your goals and values! If it doesn't, you can happily avoid all investors who use this model, and only approach those whose investment strategies and goals are in alignment with your trajectory and vision. Luckily, the vast majority of investors do not use the VC model.

Occasionally (especially if you live near Silicon Valley), you will encounter someone who is dismissive of any business that does not choose the VC route and instead chooses to stay on a path of slow and steady growth. Sometimes, they will refer to your business as a "lifestyle business," which is not meant as a compliment. This term implies that high-growth businesses are the only ones worthy of attention and respect, which is ridiculous. There are millions of non-high-growth businesses that make major contributions to their communities and generate great profits. If they all disappeared tomorrow, believe me, the world would not be a nice place to live. Yes, we could all still send each other chats on our smartphones, but where would we go to have coffee with a friend or get our dog groomed? If someone calls your business a lifestyle business, you can simply smile, secure in the knowledge that you know a lot more than he does about the options available and that you have chosen an option that will allow you to be true to your goals and values. If you still need more reassurance, Google the keywords "VC horror stories" to hear about some of the unpleasant experiences founders have had with the VC model.

The key is to *first* decide on your business goals and *then* find investors who are aligned with your goals (and design your offering accordingly). Far too many entrepreneurs design their business goals to fit the VC model, often because they don't know that there are other ways to raise capital.

Now that you know better, write down in detail your goals for your business based on what makes you happy and fulfilled, not on what you think investors want!

HOW MUCH TO RAISE

Getting clear on your business goals will help you determine how much money you should raise from investors.

Figuring out how much to raise is not always easy. If you raise too much, it can be hard to meet your obligations to your investors. If you raise too little, you can run out of money before you achieve the next milestone required for survival and growth.

Your decision about the amount to raise should be driven by your reasonable projections and desired growth rate and not by things like minimums set by investors or pressure to grow faster than is right for you.

The good news is that the amount that you decide you want to raise is not set in stone. You can adjust the number up or down later. But it's important to start with an informed estimate of the right amount for you. You may also want to consider a range. There may be a certain minimum amount that you know you need to raise to reach your goals. But there may be some "nice to haves" that would help you reach your goals faster or more easily. In that case, you may want to specify a minimum and a maximum capital raising goal. There are some kinds of raises ("raise" is a shorthand way of referring to a capital raising effort) for which the regulators may actually require you to set a minimum amount, and you will not be allowed to touch the money until you have reached that minimum. We'll discuss this in greater detail in step 4.

Financial Projections

Financial projections are a way to help you predict roughly what will happen to your business financially over the next several years. You can create various scenarios so that you can see what would happen if prices on a certain input go up, if you attract fewer customers than you're hoping for, and so on.

Many businesses, especially when they are first starting out, can face a negative cash flow situation. This is perfectly normal! It is inherent in many business models that cash will go negative before it can go positive. For example, my client CERO Cooperative wanted to start a recycling and composting business. Revenues would come from fees paid by its customers. But the company could not start providing services to customers until it bought a truck. The purchase of the truck meant that cash had to be spent before any cash came in from customers.

I know too many entrepreneurs who feel as though they have failed when they have negative cash flow in their businesses. But this is often an indication not of failure but of a need to invest money up front in order to reap the rewards of customer revenue later, a very normal state of affairs for a business. This very common situation is exactly why most businesses need investors. This is also why businesses can fail due to lack of capital. Great business ideas almost always require an up-front investment to succeed. The up-front investment may be in equipment, marketing, a sales team, legal services, a million other things—why do so many entrepreneurs seem to think that spending money on these kinds of things is a luxury? These expenditures are often essential for a business to make it. Hint Water, a very successful business that sells flavored bottled water, took eleven years to break even. The founder, Kara Goldin, thought it was more important to build a great company and a great brand than to skimp on employee benefits, excellent marketing, high-quality ingredients, and so on.[20]

So take a look at your financial projections. If you don't have any yet, stop reading right now and go to the readers' resources website (see the resources section at the end of the book for details) to download my simple financial projection template and create your projections. Do not skimp on the things you need in order to have a successful business! Of course don't include things that are not essential, such as a foosball table for the break room. But be realistic about what it will take to achieve your goals. Don't always go for the cheapest option, either—use a high-quality web designer, accountant, and lawyer. Saving money on these items now will just create expensive headaches in the future. And for goodness' sake, include a salary for yourself! It doesn't have to be high, but it should be enough for someone to live decently given your local cost of living. Also, although this book does not cover employment law, I strongly advise against using unpaid interns. When someone works for you, he or she is likely to be considered an employee under the law and therefore needs to be paid at least minimum wage. (You also need to comply with numerous other employment law requirements; it is not worth taking chances on this stuff. A lawsuit from a former unpaid intern is the last thing you want to deal with. Hire a knowledgeable employment lawyer or HR consultant.) So build salaries into your projections for everyone who works for you.

Now you have your financial projections, and you may see that in the first several years of business, your expenses exceed your revenues. As I said before, that is fine and perfectly normal, as long as you can see a pathway to eventually breaking even. Your projections just tell you how much money you will need to raise from investors. If you can estimate how much of a shortfall you have before you reach **breakeven,** you know that you probably need to raise about that amount to be able to keep the doors open and not run out of cash.

Financial projections also help you see what kinds of returns you can offer to your investors. We'll be talking more about this in step 3.

What Do You Need?

Another approach you can use for determining how much you need to raise is to think about what you need to purchase to take your business to where you want it to be and how much that will cost. Here is an exercise to help you do that.

1. Make a detailed list of the things you need to buy and the people you need to hire over the next year or two that you cannot cover with current cash flow (or other resources such as barter).

2. Put dollar amounts next to what you listed in the first step. Add an additional 10–20 percent to cover unexpected contingencies.
3. How will buying those new things and hiring those new people affect your business? For example, if you hire two new sales reps, will that lead to more expenses, such as having to hire a COO? If so, add those expenses to the list.
4. Consider creating more than one scenario. For example, if you focus on one line of business versus another, your needs will be different. Create multiple scenarios for each possibility. It is often best to choose the scenario that allows you to achieve breakeven while raising the lowest possible amount of money. You can also create scenarios for different amounts—you may want to raise a minimum of $300,000, but you should also consider what a larger amount could make possible and consider setting a "stretch goal."

The table here is an example of what this exercise might look like for a tech company:

Item	Low (items that I can't do without)	Medium (important but not essential)	High (nice to have)
Marketing campaign	$75,000	$100,000	$200,000
Sales rep (1 year)	$75,000	$75,000	$75,000
Programmer (1 year)	$100,000	$100,000	$100,000

Item	Low (items that I can't do without)	Medium (important but not essential)	High (nice to have)
Salary increase for CEO (1 year)		$25,000	$50,000
Administrative assistant (1 year)		$65,000	$65,000
Rent for larger office (1 year)			$60,000
Professional video			$25,000
Contingency (20%)	$50,000	$73,000	$115,000
TOTAL	$300,000	$438,000	$690,000

In this example, you have determined that you need to raise a minimum of $300,000, but if you could raise up to $690,000, you might be able to achieve your goals more quickly. Of course, if raising $690,000 results in an obligation to your investors that you fear you won't be able to meet, it may be best to stick with the lower number.

Note that this example does not include a line item for covering your projected cash shortfall before you break even—be sure to add that if needed!

Raising More Than One Round

What if you think you will need $5 million over the next ten years to grow your company to its ideal size? Should you try to raise all $5 million now? Or should you raise a smaller amount now and then do another round of capital raising later? The rule of thumb is that it can take six to eighteen months to reach a fundraising goal, so it is best to raise the amount you need to be able to stay in business for the next eighteen months to two years. It is usually far easier to raise $500,000 now and $4.5 million two years from now than to try to raise $5 million in one chunk. This is because two years from now, you will likely have made progress and achieved some milestones, which will make your company more attractive to investors. Also, a lot can change in two years. Maybe in two years you'll have broken even, and you won't need to raise any more capital after all.

How Much?

The exercises in this section have, I hope, helped you identify the target amount for your raise, or a range. Write this number down, as well as the methodology you used to arrive at it. The amount can always change later, but it is very helpful to have a figure to work with as you are designing your strategy.

STAYING ON TRACK

I hope you have used the materials in this step to do a lot of thinking and writing about your goals and values for the present and future of your business. Treat this writing as your bible or manifesto and check back frequently to make sure that your capital raising strategy and implementation are aligned with your core goals and values.

identify the right investors for you

As discussed in part 1, when people picture an investor, many imagine a middle-aged white man in a suit or the standard Silicon Valley uniform—khakis and a button-down shirt. I have a colleague who calls investors "the suits."

This is not at all an accurate picture of the typical investor. In fact, there is no such thing as a "typical investor." Investors are so diverse that it is impossible to generalize about them.

We will, though, talk about general categories of investors and the various kinds of relationships you can have with them so that you can get clear on which investors are right for you.

TYPES OF INVESTORS

The reason that so many people picture someone in a suit when thinking about the typical investor is that they are picturing someone whom I referred to earlier as a professional investor. A professional investor is someone who spends a majority of his or her waking hours focused on investing. Some of the categories of professional investors include venture capitalists, people who manage various kinds of investment funds, and people who manage investing for foundations and wealthy families.

Venture Capitalists

Let's take a moment to talk again about venture capitalists. As I mentioned earlier, this category of investor gets a lot of attention and praise. There is a common belief that venture capitalists earn their very high fees by providing outsized returns to those who invest in their funds (known as limited partners or LPs). Here are some truths about VC investing:[21]

+ For more than a decade, the stock markets have outperformed most VC funds.
+ Since 1997, less cash has been returned to VC investors than they have invested.
+ Fund performance declines as fund size increases above $250 million.

Although there may be a few very high profile successes in the VC world each year, the vast majority of companies that VCs invest in do not meet the VC's target minimum return. Unless you think you can realistically meet VC expectations (on average, they want the company to increase in value by at least tenfold in five to seven years), this is not a good source of capital for you to pursue. And if you do not think you can meet VC expectations, you are in very good company, because it is a rare business that can.

Angel Investors

What about angel investors?

I define an angel investor as a high-net-worth individual (someone who is accredited—see chapter 3 in part 1 for details on what this means) who invests his or her own money (unlike venture capitalists, who invest other people's money).

Some are "active angels" who spend a large amount of time on investing and often join angel groups. I include these kinds of angels in the professional investor category. According to the Angel Capital Association, about 8 percent of accredited investors are active angels.[22] The other 92 percent are people who meet the definition of an accredited investor but do not actively invest in small businesses. I include those folks in the category of nonprofessional investors.

Professional Investors

About how many professional investors are there in the United States? If we define professional investors as active angels and people who get paid to invest other people's money (venture capitalists, fund managers, wealth managers, and private equity investors), the total number of professional investors is in the neighborhood of 350,000 (approximately 300,000 active angels,[23] 1,200 VC funds,[24] 4,200 private equity firms,[25] and 6,000 family offices,[26] and let's say about 35,000 miscellaneous professional investors).

Nonprofessional Investors

The adult population of the United States is about 250 million. Professional investors therefore make up about .1 percent of the total population.

Not all adults in the United States are potential investors. Someone who is living in poverty or close to poverty is unlikely to be able to make an investment. However, a majority of the US adult population is made up of investors. These are people who have investments in stocks, bonds, mutual funds, and so on: 60 percent of households have retirement investments,[27] 44 percent of households invest in mutual funds,[28] and 52 percent of Americans invest in the stock market.[29] And, of course, many more have funds invested in depository accounts at banks. If we were to estimate conservatively that half of the adult population has investments, that would mean that there are more than 120 million investors in the United States. So of all of the investors in the United States, only about .3 percent are professional investors.

Would you rather try to chase after that tiny percentage of the population to raise money, or reach out to everybody—the 100 percent?

So who are these millions of investors whom we call nonprofessional investors? For starters, we can divide them into two categories: accredited and unaccredited. Only a few million people in the United States are accredited. The vast majority are unaccredited. As I mentioned in chapter 3, many lawyers and advisors will tell you that you should not talk to unaccredited investors when raising money. But, as you can see, this would mean that you have to leave out tens of millions of potential investors! Why would you do that?

According to Michael Shuman, "Americans' long-term savings in stocks, bonds, mutual funds, pension funds, and life insurance funds total about $30 trillion. But not even 1 percent of these savings touch local small business—even though roughly half the jobs and the output in the private economy come from them."[30]

This is a huge opportunity! Many investors would like to find a way to diversify their investments and shift at least some small portion out of Wall Street and into Main Street. By raising money for your business from the 100 percent, you can allow people to do just that.

NARROWING IT DOWN

Now that you know that about half of the adult population could be a potential investor, how do you narrow down your options and focus on the ones who are right for you?

First, let's talk about why it is so important to narrow down your options. You might be thinking, well, if everyone can invest, why don't I just ask everyone to invest? Some of the wisdom from the world of marketing applies to raising capital as well: if you are marketing to everyone, you are marketing to no one. It is far more effective to target potential investors who fit your particular goals and values than to use a spray-and-pray approach (that is, asking everyone and her brother to invest and pray that someone says yes). You have only so much time and energy, so use it to connect with the people who are most likely to say yes *and* whom you are most likely to love having as an investor.

Who Are Your Ideal Investors?

Your ideal investors are people who are passionate about the same things you are. They are people who totally "get it" within the first few moments of hearing your vision. They are people who believe in you and want to see you and your business succeed.

The clearer you are about your ideal investors and the type of relationship you would like to have with them, the easier it will be to find those people. So, let's dig in to some exercises to help you identify your ideal investors.

Create Your Ideal Investor Profile

Your ideal investor is someone who will really appreciate and value the unique mix of benefits that come from being a part of your business.

Picture who that person or people might be. Remember, these people do not have to be professional investors. They can be people who attend your place of worship. They can be your customers. They can be your suppliers. They can be people who are passionate about what you're doing. They can be a combination of these and many other possibilities.

Make a list of three to five people who could be your ideal investor. They may be actual people or imaginary people. Give each imaginary person a name. Remember, even investors that are institutions, such as family offices or foundations, are represented by individual people, so go ahead and include representatives of organizational investors in your list if you like.

Write each person's name at the top of a blank sheet of paper and write down everything you can think of about that person, including what would make him or her an ideal investor. Be sure to include both demographics (e.g., age and geographic location) and psychographics (personality characteristics).

Also make a list of what you *don't* want in an investor. Here are some examples:

+ Very opinionated—thinks she is always right
+ Dishonest, not trustworthy
+ Does not communicate clearly

Once you have a clear picture in your mind of one or more ideal investors, choose one and pretend for a moment that you are that person. Really try to imagine what it is like to be him or her. What is she looking for in an investment opportunity? What is important to her? What gets her excited? What does she find irritating? What are her biggest dreams and aspirations? Write all of the insights that come to you from putting yourself in her shoes.

Your Relationship with Your Investors

What kind of relationship do you want to have with your investors? There are actually many options, regardless of the type of investment you offer. There is a myth that I hear repeated in the start-up advising community that if you offer equity, you have to give up control. This is simply not true. Some kinds of investors will expect to get some control of your business. Venture capitalists are well known for this, which is why it is often said that when you bring on a venture capitalist, you are actually hiring your boss. But not all investors want control.

Do you want your investors to be your boss? Do you want to give up any control at all? On the one hand, giving up some degree of control in exchange for something very valuable, such as access to a high level of industry expertise and contacts, can be worthwhile. On the other hand, it could be preferable to use the money you raise to hire someone to provide that expertise. That way, you can fire him or her if you don't like the advice you're getting. It's not nearly as easy to fire an investor!

Here are some of the options for the kinds of relationships you can have with investors:

+ The investor is basically your boss with the ability to fire you.
+ The investor has voting rights, but is equal to you in terms of decision-making authority.
+ The investor has voting rights, but you have ultimate authority over major decisions.
+ The investor has no voting rights, but serves as an advisor with whom you can talk on a regular basis.
+ The investor has no voting rights at all and is very hands-off, but is available to support you when you ask.

Picture your relationship with your investor(s). How do you feel when you spend time with them? What makes the relationship supportive and fulfilling? Do you see them every day in your office, or do you see them once a year at your big company gala? Or something in between?

Write down in as much detail as possible what you would like your relationship with your investors to look like.

How Do You Find Them?

Your ideal investors are people who value a lot of the same things you do. So if you think about where and how *you* spend your time, it is likely that some of those places and activities are ones that your ideal investors also enjoy.

Ask yourself the following questions:

+ Where do I go where I instantly feel at home and comfortable?
+ What publications and online communities do I like because they speak to what is important and interesting to me?
+ What organizations offer trainings, workshops, and retreats that I would love to attend?
+ To what nonprofits would I love to be able to make donations because I am so passionate about their mission?
+ Where do I love to go on vacation, and what activities do I love doing when I'm not working?

Some of your answers may include things that are a financial stretch. Maybe you would love to go to a meditation retreat at a certain luxury spa, but you have always assumed you couldn't afford it. If you think of the retreat as a way not only to do something you love but also to meet like-minded people who might be thrilled to hear about the opportunity to invest in your business, maybe the cost starts to look like a worthy investment toward the fulfillment of your most cherished dreams.

Another way to think about where you might find your potential investors is to think about who benefits from the success of your business. Your customers love you and want you to be successful; they might be interested in becoming investors. Your suppliers' financial well-being is tied directly to yours; maybe some of them would be interested in investing. If your business is solving a problem that has a natural constituency, the members of that constituency might be interested in investing. For example, if your company produces renewable energy, it is very likely that environmentalists could be potential investors. Maybe you could go to a local Sierra Club meeting or a gathering of electric car enthusiasts and connect with some potential investors.

Field Work

By now, you've created one or more profiles of your ideal investors. Now is the time to go out and gather data. Make a list of three to five people who could be ideal investors for you. Invite them out for lunch or coffee or set up a phone meeting. Tell them you are doing some research about the future of your business and would really appreciate their input because you value their perspective.

At the meeting, after you've broken the ice, tell them that you have a list of some questions you would like to ask them. (This assumes they already know about your business. If they don't, take a few minutes to describe it.) Here is your script:

> I am thinking about raising money from investors for
> my business. I'm not raising money now, but I am doing
> some thinking about the best way to go about it. I really
> wanted to talk to you because I value your opinion, and

I think you could help me make some decisions about what fundraising strategy to pursue. So here are my questions:

+ If I were to raise money for my business, what kinds of people do you think would be interested in investing?
+ Imagine that I was approaching you as a potential investor. What would be your biggest questions or concerns about investing?
+ What would be exciting or interesting to you about investing?
+ What kind of financial return would you be looking for?
+ What kind of investment would you be most interested in making? For example, would you want to own a piece of the company (equity), would you want to make a loan (debt), or would you want to make some other kind of investment? [Some people will not know the answer to this question, which is fine.]
+ How long would you be willing to have the money tied up before you could get it back out?
+ Are there any special considerations related to tax that you would be concerned about? For example, do you like to generate passive losses from your investments to offset gains? Do you prefer not having to deal with K-1s [the tax forms you receive when you're an equity investor in a pass-through entity like an S Corp]?
+ What kinds of things could I do to make the investment more attractive [higher return, perks, discounts, community, etc.]?

- What do you like and not like about where your money is currently invested?
- Do you know anyone else who might be willing to answer these questions to help with my research?

Of course, you can modify this based on the person's level of sophistication, how well you know him or her, and other factors.

YOUR IDEAL INVESTORS ARE OUT THERE!

Be prepared to spend a significant amount of time identifying your ideal investors, and approach the task with curiosity and an open mind. You may start out with a few people who you think will be perfect and then realize by talking to them that they actually aren't that excited about your idea. That is great! The more you go out and talk to people and try new sources of potential investors, the more quickly you will find the right people. If your first few conversations don't go well, remember that this is all part of the learning process, and keep going. I know many successful business owners who have met with a hundred investors or more before finding the right ones. Whatever you do, don't give up!

design your offer

Now is the time to figure out how you want to compensate investors. In other words, how will your investors get their money back plus something additional to compensate them for parking their money with you? In legal terminology, what kind of security will you be offering?

Many business owners go to their lawyer or advisor and ask for help raising money from investors. Often, the lawyer or advisor will hand them something called a *convertible note* and tell them to go out and offer this to their investors.

A convertible note is one type of security that you can offer, but there are numerous other options. You should never start offering an investment opportunity (i.e., security) to potential investors without first understanding all of the options available and the implications of each. The type of security you offer will have major effects on you and your business down the road, including how much control and ownership you give up, what kinds of taxes you and your investors have to pay, what your investors expect, and your ability to raise additional rounds of capital.

You want to choose a security that has the greatest likelihood of (1) creating alignment between your goals and interests and those of your investors and (2) fulfilling on its promises. Every security contains a set of promises that you are making to your investor. These promises may be explicit, such as the promise to pay a certain amount of interest each year, or implicit. For example, when an investor purchases equity in your company, depending on the terms of the equity, there may be an implicit promise that you will work as hard as you can to make sure the company is sold at as high a price as possible so that the equity investor can make a financial return.

This step gives you a detailed process to help you decide what type of security to offer. You can design your security almost any way you want—you can get quite creative! Please note, however, that the more creative you are, the more important it is to work with an experienced lawyer *and* a very knowledgeable tax advisor. Although this can cost some money, you are far better off ensuring that you have designed your offering in a way that fits with your goals and values than using an off-the-shelf boilerplate document that can cause major headaches down the road.

A NOTE ABOUT THIS STEP

Because there are so many different types of investments you can offer, this part of the book is quite long. I recommend reading the whole step to get a general idea of all of the possibilities and then go back and read more carefully the parts that apply to your situation.

Fasten your seat belt and get ready to learn about the numerous ways that investors can be compensated!

We will go through the following decision points:

1. Understand how your business structure and tax status affect what you can offer to investors. Decide whether you need to change your structure or tax status to be able to raise money the way you want to.
2. Choose an instrument.
3. Choose what economic rights your investors will have.
4. Choose what governance rights your investors will have.
5. Add some perks to sweeten the deal.

DECISION POINT 1: UNDERSTAND YOUR STRUCTURE AND DECIDE WHETHER IT IS THE RIGHT ONE FOR YOU

When entrepreneurs start a business, they usually form some kind of entity—often an LLC or corporation—and they select a tax status. Unfortunately, the structure and tax status they choose are not always consistent with the capital raising strategy that is best for them. This section discusses the various structures and their implications for raising capital. Once you have worked through it, you may decide to change your structure and/or tax status before beginning the capital raising process.

What is the legal structure of your business? Here are the main possibilities:

+ Sole proprietorship or partnership (this means that you haven't filed any entity formation documents with a state government)
+ Corporation
+ Limited liability company (LLC)
+ Nonprofit organization (usually a type of corporation)
+ Cooperative

If you have formed an entity, under what state law was it formed?

How is your business taxed? Is it an S Corp or C Corp? Is it taxed like a partnership? Exempt from tax because it conducts charitable and educational activities?

In this section, we will discuss the implications of all of these structure and tax choices (possibly made many years ago without complete information) for your capital raising strategy. On the basis of what you learn, you may decide to make some changes to better fit with your chosen capital raising strategy. If so, be sure to check with a lawyer and tax expert, because switching from one type of entity to another can have unexpected legal and tax consequences.

Sole Proprietorships and Partnerships

If you never filed papers with a state government to create a legal entity for your business, you have either a sole proprietorship (if you are just one person) or a partnership (if you are two or more people). A sole proprietorship can raise money from investors in the form of loans, but not equity.

A partnership can raise money in the form of loans and can also bring on additional partners who can purchase equity in the partnership.

If you want to raise money from investors, it is generally recommended that you go ahead and form some kind of entity. The formation of an entity allows you to protect your personal assets in case something goes wrong. Corporations and LLCs have something called *limited liability*, which means that owners of these entities generally don't put their personal assets (e.g., their home or car) at risk. If the entity defaults on a loan or loses a lawsuit, the owners can lose their entire investment in the company, but their personal assets (in most cases) will be shielded from liability. Another reason to form an entity before raising money from investors is that it gives you a lot more options for how you can bring in investors. Finally, it makes you look more serious about your business because you have invested the resources necessary to create a formal structure.

Taxation of Sole Proprietorships and Partnerships

Sole proprietorships and partnerships are "disregarded" for tax purposes. This means that the sole proprietorship or partnership is not itself taxed, and all tax items are passed through to the owners. So at the end of the company's fiscal year, the company's accountant closes the books and figures out if the company made a profit or loss and whether there are any other tax items to report. These items are passed through to the owners of the company, and they fill them in on their personal tax returns. This pass-through tax treatment is available for other kinds of entities as well, as discussed in detail later.

Corporations

A corporation is an independent legal entity, separate from the people who own it. You form a corporation by choosing a state where you want to incorporate and filing a document called the Articles of Incorporation or the Certificate of Incorporation with the state government. The state statute under which you form your corporation lays out various requirements, such as the number of people you must have on your board of directors, what officers you must have, how you have to give notice for shareholders' meetings, and the like. Corporate statutes are very similar from state to state—the corporate structure was invented hundreds of years ago and generally includes the same basic building blocks regardless of the state. These building blocks include a board of directors that has ultimate responsibility for all corporate decisions; officers (usually a president, secretary, and treasurer), who may or may not be board members but who are chosen by the board to manage the corporation; and the owners of the corporation, who are called *shareholders* or *stockholders*.

The ownership of a corporation is divided up into shares of stock. Generally speaking, the number of shares you own divided by the total number of outstanding shares that have been issued (i.e., sold to shareholders) represents the percentage of the company that you own. For example, if you own 300,000 shares, your cofounder owns 200,000 shares, and no one else owns any shares, you own 60 percent of the corporation, and your cofounder owns 40 percent. The shareholders with voting rights elect the board of directors.

Corporations can offer different types of stock to investors. Different types of stock are called *classes* (or sometimes *series*). So, for example, you could have a class of voting stock and a class of nonvoting stock.

All corporations have *common stock*. This is the stock that is issued to the founders when they first form the new company. Common stock is very simple and usually comes with the right to vote (one share, one vote).

Benefit Corporations and Social Purpose Corporations

Over the last several years, there has been a movement to create new corporate statutes that are designed to allow corporate leaders to consider the interests of all stakeholders (workers, suppliers, customers, the environment, the community, and so on) when making decisions, without fear of getting sued by shareholders. This movement was spurred by stories of mission-driven public companies (e.g., Ben & Jerry's) that were pressured by shareholders to sell the company to the highest bidder even though the founders feared that the mission of the company would be compromised by the sale.

Approximately thirty states have adopted these statutes, known as *benefit corporation, social purpose corporation,* or *public benefit corporation statutes.*

Companies formed under these statutes have the same options in terms of the types of securities they can offer and are taxed in the same way as regular corporations. The primary difference between these corporate forms and plain vanilla corporations is that the board of directors has more protection if it makes a decision in the name of public or environmental benefit that shareholders do not consider to be in their best financial interest. These companies are generally required to be evaluated pursuant to a third-party standard to demonstrate that they have a public benefit or social purpose.

Whether you form your company as a regular corporation, a benefit corporation, or a social purpose corporation, there is no effect on the tax treatment of the business or its shareholders.

Taxation of Corporations

C Corps

The default rule under federal tax law is that corporations are taxed under Subchapter C of the Internal Revenue Code.

If the corporation is taxed under Subchapter C (i.e., is a *C Corp*), the company's profits are taxed at the corporate level at corporate tax rates. If the company pays out a share of the profits (dividends) to its shareholders, the shareholders have to pay income tax on the dividends. This is known as the "double tax" because the same profits are taxed twice— once at the entity level and then at the individual shareholder level when they are paid out as dividends. Note, however, that dividends are often taxed at a lower rate than the regular income tax rates.

S Corps

Many smaller corporations elect to be taxed under Subchapter S of the Internal Revenue Code because it allows them to avoid the double tax.

If the corporation is taxed under Subchapter S (i.e., is an *S Corp*), the company's profits are taxed at the shareholder level and not at the entity level. This means that regardless of whether the company pays dividends, the shareholders have to pay tax on their share of the company profits. If the company has a loss, it may be deductible on the shareholders' tax returns. This type of taxation is called *pass-through* because the tax items are "passed through" to the shareholders. The company must issue a K-1 form to its shareholders every year to tell them what they must report on their taxes. Paying dividends to the investors does not affect the amount of income tax they have to pay because the investors pay tax on their **pro rata** share of the company profits, not on the actual cash they receive.

Many investors do not like pass-through taxation because it makes the preparation of their personal taxes more complicated and because of the risk that they will have to pay tax on profits they do not actually receive (known as the "phantom income" problem). At the same time, investors who have passive gains on other investments may like the idea of investing in an early-stage S Corp that is making losses, because the investor may be able to use the losses to offset the gains from other investments.

Taxation under Subchapter S can be very favorable in some circumstances, depending on the shareholders' individual tax situations. There are some limitations on whether a corporation is allowed to elect taxation under Subchapter S:

+ An S Corp cannot have more than one class of stock (unless the only difference between the classes is their voting rights)—in other words, all shareholders must have the same economic rights.

+ Only individuals and not entities can be shareholders in S Corps.
+ Only US citizens or permanent residents can be shareholders in S Corps.
+ There is a cap on the number of shareholders an S Corp can have (one hundred).

Limited Liability Companies (LLCs)

LLCs are not corporations. They are a fairly recently invented entity that combines the limited liability protection of a corporation and the flexibility of a partnership. You form an LLC by choosing a state where you want to form and filing a document called the Articles of Organization or the Certificate of Formation with the state government. The state statute under which you form your LLC lays out various requirements governing the LLC, which are much fewer than for a corporation. Under state LLC law, you can write almost anything you want into the LLC's internal governing document (known as the operating agreement). You can have multiple classes of equity, each with different rights, and you can also be creative with how the LLC is governed. Unlike corporations, LLCs are not required to have a board of directors, officers, or even meetings.

The equity interests in an LLC are called *memberships* or *membership interests*. From time to time, you may also hear them referred to as *units*. Generally, you would not use the term *share* or *stock* when referring to an equity interest in an LLC.

LLC Taxation

The default type of taxation for an LLC is taxation under Subchapter K (partnership taxation). Subchapter K provides for pass-through treatment for the tax items of the entity. Remember, S Corps also have pass-through treatment, but the two subchapters do have some differences. For example, with partnership taxation (Subchapter K), everyone who owns an equity interest in the LLC who also works for the LLC has to pay self-employment tax on all income from the LLC, regardless of whether it is called a salary or profit sharing. Under Subchapter S, dividends paid to shareholders who work for the company are not subject to employment tax.

This is why some LLCs elect to be taxed under Subchapter S instead of Subchapter K. They can also elect to be taxed under Subchapter C (or Subchapter T if the LLC operates like a cooperative—see the next section for details).

Co-ops

Co-ops are very diverse because each state co-op statute is different. Many states have more than one co-op statute governing different types of co-ops. Generally, the equity owners of a co-op are called *members*. The members of the co-op include "patrons" of the co-op. The term *patron* applies to anyone who does business with the co-op, which can include customers, producers, or workers, or a combination of multiple kinds of patrons. However, co-ops can generally have nonpatrons as equity investors (i.e., members) as well.

One of the considerations for co-ops when raising money from investors is the importance of ensuring that the patron members remain in control. (This usually means that they have the right to elect a majority of the board of directors and to have final say over major decisions such as sale of the company, merger, or the choice to convert to another type of entity.) Most cooperative statutes do not allow outside investors to choose a majority of the board or have other rights to control the cooperative. Many state co-op statutes also limit the financial returns that can be paid to outside investors.

Cooperative Taxation

There is a section of the tax code called Subchapter T that is designed to be used by co-ops. Subchapter T provides a beneficial treatment of dividends that are paid to patrons—unlike dividends paid to investors, patronage dividends are not subject to the double tax. Some co-ops elect to be taxed under Subchapter T; others may choose a different tax treatment. Recently, a new type of cooperative structure has been adopted in several states called the *limited cooperative association* (LCA). Many co-ops formed as LCAs elect to be taxed under Subchapter K (partnership tax).

Nonprofits

Nonprofit organizations are usually a special kind of corporation that is just like a regular corporation except that it does not have the ability to issue stock. In other words, a nonprofit cannot be owned by anyone. Unlike in a corporation, in which the shareholders choose the board, in a non-profit, the board itself elects new board members. (Some nonprofits have voting members who elect the board, but this is not very common.)

Because a nonprofit does not have any ownership interests, it can only raise money from investors in the form of debt; it cannot offer an equity investment.

There may be some other limitations on what a nonprofit can offer to investors depending on the details of the statute under which it was formed. For example, in California, a majority of the board of a charitable nonprofit must be people who do not receive any compensation from the nonprofit. This means that it would be illegal for a majority of the board to be investors in the nonprofit.

Nonprofit Taxation

The default rule is that nonprofits are taxed just like any corporation, but the majority of nonprofits apply for federal tax-exempt status. There are many different categories of federal tax-exempt status. The most well-known is tax exemption under Section 501(c)(3), which is available for charitable and educational organizations. Tax-exempt status usually means that the nonprofit is prohibited from compensating anyone at a level that would be considered above market rate. This includes investors, so the nonprofit would want to be careful to do some research about comparable investment opportunities and the interest rates they are offering before designing the debt instrument they plan to offer to investors.

Your Decision

Now that you've read the discussion in decision point 1, do you think that your current structure and tax status are right for you? If you're still not sure, don't worry, because as you work through the rest of this step and narrow down the type of investment you want to offer, you will be able to determine whether what you want to offer fits with your current structure and tax status. In step 4, you'll make some additional decisions that may also guide your choices about structure and tax status.

DECISION POINT 2: CHOOSE AN INSTRUMENT

Here is your first big decision: Equity or debt?

I wish I could tell you that there are more options than equity or debt, but your accountant and the IRS would beg to differ. Because of tax and accounting rules, every type of investment must be classified as one or the other.

This can create a bit of a hassle because sometimes you want to get really creative and design an instrument that has some characteristics more commonly associated with debt (e.g., the ability for investors to get their money back out after a certain period of time) and others more commonly associated with equity (e.g., prohibiting payments to investors until your bank and other lenders receive what is due to them). These creative instruments can be great to offer to investors, but it is necessary to work with an attorney and a tax expert to prevent potential problems down the road. For example, let's say you offer a debt instrument, and the right of your investors to get paid back is somewhat uncertain because it depends on your ability to reach certain revenue goals. It is possible that the IRS could look at this and say, "This actually looks more like equity to us; we are going to recharacterize it as equity." Then all of a sudden, all those tax deductions you took for interest payments will be disallowed because the IRS says they were not interest after all.

What Is Debt?

Debt is a binding promise to pay back the investment. The initial investment becomes the principal, and you pay back the principal plus interest.

Debt is evidenced with a promissory note.

Debt is an instrument that can be used regardless of your business structure. It can be offered by a sole proprietorship, a partnership, a nonprofit, a co-op, a corporation, and an LLC. Because it does not affect the ownership of your business, debt is generally much simpler to document than an equity investment.

Debt sits on your company balance sheet as a liability. If you have a large liability on your balance sheet and not a lot of cash contributed in the form of equity from the company founders (or donors in the case of a nonprofit), this can make investors nervous. Many investors like to see a healthy balance of both debt and equity invested in the company. Also, if you have a lot of investment in the form of debt and not a lot of equity, it can be difficult to get a line of credit, a real estate loan, or any other kind of loan from a bank or institutional lender. Another downside of debt is that there is usually a fixed schedule of payments you have to make. If your business is going to take a long time to break even, making those payments may not be possible—though of course this depends on the specific provisions of the debt instrument (which we will discuss in more detail in the next decision point).

What Are the Tax Implications of Debt?

Interest payments are tax deductible to the **issuer** (i.e., the company that is borrowing the money). The investor pays income tax on interest she receives at her regular income tax rate. Following the end of each accounting year, the issuer must provide a Form 1099-INT to its investors showing how much interest was paid.

What Is Equity?

Equity is an ownership interest in the issuer. As already noted, equity cannot be offered by sole proprietorships or nonprofits.

From the investor's perspective, equity is riskier than debt because it is generally not required to be paid back, and companies are only allowed to pay profit distributions to equity holders when they are solvent. (The details of when profit distributions can be paid vary somewhat from state to state.) And creditors (i.e., holders of debt instruments) are first in line to get paid back if the company goes out of business.

Equity investors usually have the right to receive certain information about the company in which they own equity. (This is spelled out in the state statute under which your entity is formed and possibly in your formation documents.) Sometimes equity investors have voting rights, but this is generally not required. Voting rights usually mean the right to elect the governing body and to vote on major decisions, such as dissolution, sale, or merger.

Equity is generally more complicated to document than debt. For example, with a corporation, you may have to amend your articles of incorporation before you can offer equity to investors; with an LLC, you may have to amend your operating agreement, whereas debt does not require amending any of your organizational documents.

Also, something that makes equity a bit more complicated is that there is no way to sell equity without giving it a price. That is why you will sometimes hear the sale of equity referred to as a "priced round." Equity always has to have a price. How do you figure out how to price your equity? You could hire a professional valuator to help you decide on a price. This is very expensive, however, and really not practical when you are at an early stage because it is so hard to figure out what a company is really worth when it is just starting out. You can also use a valuation calculator. (I have provided one for you on the readers' resources website—see the resources section of this book for details.) Or you can pull a number out of a hat. The key is that you and your investors have to agree on a price. Here is an example of how this can work:

Susan has formed a corporation, and she is the sole shareholder. She decides she wants to sell equity to investors. She does some projections and realizes that she probably needs to raise about $500,000. She does not want to give up more than 20 percent of the ownership of her company.

So she does the following calculation: What would my company have to be worth in order for a $500,000 investment to equal 20 percent of the total value? (Try to remember your high school algebra now!)

$500,000 = 20% of $X
To solve for X: X = $500,000 divided by
20% = $2,500,000

So the value of the company will be $2.5 million *after* the $500,000 has been invested. This is called the *post-money valuation*. The post-money valuation equals the value of the company before the equity investment is made (i.e., the pre-money valuation) plus the amount of the equity investment.

What is the pre-money valuation (the value of the company before it has received any investment)? It is the post-money valuation minus the investment; in this case, the pre-money valuation is $2.5 million minus $500,000, or $2 million.

So when Susan goes out to raise money from equity investors, she will tell her potential investors that she has set the current valuation at $2 million. Her potential investors may or may not agree with her, and they may want to negotiate on this.

Some companies prefer to delay the conversation about the valuation of the company and may therefore choose to offer *convertible notes* or similar instruments (discussed later in this step) instead of equity. Also, as I will discuss later, the valuation sometimes does not matter much at all. But that doesn't change the fact that to sell equity, you must give it a price.

What Are the Tax Implications of Equity?

The tax implications of equity vary quite a bit depending on how your entity is taxed. If your entity is taxed as a pass-through (i.e., under Subchapter S or Subchapter K), the tax items of the company will be passed through to your equity investors. So if the company has a profit, that profit will be allocated among the equity owners for tax purposes regardless of whether they receive any actual cash.

For example, let's say an S Corp has a $10,000 profit at the end of the tax year, and it has two shareholders who each own 500,000 shares of common stock. Each of the two shareholders will have to report $5,000 of revenue on his or her individual tax return. This is still the case even if the corporation does not pay out any profit distributions to the shareholders. The company's tax preparer uses the Form K-1 to provide the information the equity holders need to be able to report this on their tax return.

If the entity is not taxed as a pass-through, there is no tax consequence to the equity holders unless you pay a dividend or distribution (i.e., pay out a share of the profits). If you did make a distribution, you would issue a Form 1099-DIV to each investor, and he or she would have to pay income tax on that amount. Because the tax on dividends is generally lower than for other sources of income, many investors are very happy to get dividends. At the same time, the dividend payments are not tax deductible to the company (remember the double tax?).

What if your investor sells the equity to someone else? If she sells the equity for a price that is higher than what she originally paid, this will be treated as a taxable capital gain, which also has favorable tax treatment compared to regular income.

Other Instruments

I know I said that every instrument has to be equity or debt, but I want to address a few instruments here that have some characteristics of both (which is why they may drive your CPA crazy).

The first one is *convertible debt,* aka a convertible promissory note. This is generally treated as a debt instrument, but investors in convertible debt usually think of it more as equity. A convertible note is very popular for early-stage Silicon Valley–style tech companies.

Here is how it works: Let's say you are just starting out with a great idea. There are some angel investors who love what you are doing and want to invest. They could buy an equity stake in the company, but it is so early that it will be difficult to agree on a valuation. (See the earlier discussion about valuation in the section on equity.) But you do know that you plan to do an equity raise sometime in the next couple of years. So the early-stage investors purchase convertible notes instead of equity, with the understanding that the convertible note will convert into equity when you raise your first round of equity investment. That first round of equity investment will set the valuation as well as the terms of the equity. In exchange for coming in early, the convertible note holders get a discount on the price of the equity when the conversion happens. What if conversion doesn't happen, because you don't end up raising an equity round after all? Depending on the terms of the convertible note, you may have to pay back the note holders just as you would if it had been a straight debt investment, or the debt could convert to the same class of equity that is held by the founders (usually common stock). In a Silicon Valley–style deal, investors often think of a convertible note as an early equity investment because they are expecting the conversion to happen. But technically, if the note requires the investment to be paid back if there is no conversion, it is debt. There are lots variations on the kinds of provisions you can put into a convertible note. We will discuss those in greater detail later.

The next instrument that has characteristics of both equity and debt is something called an *agreement for future equity* (often known as a SAFE—simple agreement for future equity). This was invented to provide an alternative to the convertible note in Silicon Valley–style deals. The reasoning behind the SAFE is that Silicon Valley investors don't think of convertible notes as debt anyway, so why not more accurately reflect the thinking of the parties by simply selling the investors the right to receive equity in the future? So the investor gives money to the company in exchange for the right to receive equity at a discounted price when the company raises its first equity round. A problem with this instrument is that there is not universal agreement among accountants regarding how this should be treated from a tax perspective. There are some tax experts who are concerned that the IRS could treat the investment in a SAFE as the sale of an asset, in which case the entire investment amount would be taxable to the company. Thus SAFEs pose a risk due to the uncertainty of tax treatment. However, there are investors in Silicon Valley who are using them.

In addition to the SAFE, a few other tools based on similar reasoning have been invented. One is called the *Keep It Simple Security* (KISS). There is a debt version and equity version of the KISS. The debt version is similar to a convertible note, and the equity version is similar to the SAFE. Another tool called *convertible equity* is also similar to the SAFE. These are various attempts to defer the purchase of equity without requiring the company to offer debt.

A third type of instrument that companies use to raise money that is really neither equity nor debt is *prepayment*. This is payment for the right to receive a product or service in the future. For example, let's say I want to open a new coworking space, and I need to raise $750,000 to be able to do it. So I do a big campaign to offer everyone in my community the opportunity to buy a $10,000 one-year membership for only $9,000. The money I collect in the transaction would be taxable to my company as ordinary income because I am selling a product or service to customers (of course this would be net of expenses). Is this really a securities offering, or does it fall into a different category? That is a bit unclear. Some state courts have found these kinds of arrangements to be securities offerings. The likelihood that this would be treated as a securities offering would depend on many factors, such as how risky the investment is, whether there is any protection for the investors in case you can't deliver on your promise, and how broadly the opportunity was advertised. So if you decide to raise money using this strategy, you should consider consulting a knowledgeable securities lawyer.

Your Decision

Now that you have reviewed all of the various types of instruments, which one do you think best fits your goals: equity, debt, or one of the hybrids?

DECISION POINT 3: ECONOMIC RIGHTS

Okay! Let's assume that you have decided between equity and debt, or have chosen a convertible note, SAFE, or prepayment campaign (or some combination—you can offer more than one thing at a time). Now let's dive in to the details of the instrument you are offering. As I mentioned before, there is an infinite number of creative details you can add to your instrument! Be sure to know all the options and choose the one that works best for you.

When deciding on the economic rights you are going to offer to potential investors, go back and review the work you completed in step 1. You want to design an instrument that fits with your goals and values. For example, if you want to be able to have free time to spend with your family, don't offer an instrument that requires you to work day and night to be able to fulfill your investors' return expectations. If you are not going to break even for ten years, don't offer an instrument that requires you to make large monthly payments. Design the economic rights of your investment in a way that allows you to meet or exceed expectations without having to sacrifice your goals and values.

Options for Debt

This section describes the numerous options for structuring an offering of debt to investors. First, I describe simple loans and then some more creative structures in which the payments vary based on the performance of the company.

Simple Models

The simplest kind of debt structure is one where you say, "I am going to pay X percent annual simple interest per year for Y years and then I will pay back the principal." This can also include the right to repay early, which would allow you to end the relationship earlier than originally envisioned by paying back the investor with cash from operations or a refinance.

Here is an example of how a simple note like this would work: Let's say you borrow $10,000 each from ten investors. You give each of the investors a promissory note in which you promise to pay back the investment after five years, plus 5 percent simple interest each year. You would specify a time for the interest payment to be made—for example, within thirty days after the end of the calendar year. So, every January for four years, you pay each of the ten investors $500. (In the first year, this amount might be prorated to reflect less than a full year that the loan was outstanding.) In the fifth year, you pay each investor $10,500 (the principal plus the final interest payment). This kind of instrument is so simple that you can probably forgo working with an attorney and tax expert and just download a promissory note from a reputable online source. (Of course you still have to make sure your offering is compliant with securities law, as discussed in step 4!)

Another option is to amortize the payments. This means that you pay a larger amount, consisting of both principal and interest, each year (or other period) so that you don't have a big balloon payment due at the end of the term. To calculate the annual payment to your investors, you can use the PMT function in Microsoft Excel.

You could also defer payments for a certain period if you need time to be able to generate enough revenue to be able to pay back the loan. If you do this, it is important to consult with a tax advisor regarding compliance with special rules governing deferred interest payments.

Another option is to have a variable interest rate instead of a fixed interest rate. This is a way to protect investors in case interest rates for other investments go up. For example, if you had a ten-year note with a 5 percent interest rate and during the ten-year period when the loan was outstanding, banks started paying 7 percent, your investors would not be very happy. So you can tie your interest rate to a benchmark. Possible benchmarks include LIBOR (London Interbank Offered Rate) or the prime rate. An interesting benchmark to consider using is called *RSF Prime*. RSF Prime is an interest rate set by a non-profit organization called RSF Social Finance. It is set via a conversation between borrowers and lenders about what is fair.

Note that loans from banks and other institutional lenders usually require monthly payments, but you could offer less frequent payments, such as quarterly, biannual, or annual payments, to your investors.

Performance-Based Models

Now let's talk about some more creative models. These models vary the payments due based on the company's ability to pay. This can be a very beneficial feature for both the investor and the investee because it increases the likelihood that the company will remain solvent and aligns the interests of the two parties.

One model, called the *demand dividend* (aka a subordinated variable payment debt obligation), was invented by the Miller Center for Social Entrepreneurship at Santa Clara University. This is a loan that requires the borrower to make payments based on cash flow. Usually 25–50 percent of free cash flow (gross sales less discounts, cost of goods sold, operating expenses, and periodic payments of outstanding debt due within the reporting period) is paid to the lender each period. These payments are made for an indefinite period of time until a fixed payoff amount is reached. The payoff amount is usually between 1.5 and 2 times the original investment amount. There may be a "honeymoon period" of ten to twenty-four months at the beginning of the term in which the company is not required to make any payments. Note also that unless there is positive cash flow, no payment is due.

There are many variations on this general idea of a variable payment based on the company's performance and a set payoff amount with no specified time frame for reaching that payoff amount. Here are the main choices to consider:

1. What is the amount of the regular payment? This could be a percentage of free cash flow, as in the de-

mand dividend model, or it could be a percentage of gross revenues, gross margin (gross revenues less cost of sales), operating profit (aka EBITDA—earnings before interest, taxes, depreciation, and amortization), and the like. You can also subtract certain items out of the number to which the percentage is applied, such as customer returns and refunds or customer payments for shipping. Ideally, this will be a number that is easily ascertained and verified. On the one hand, gross revenue is the easiest number to use because it can be determined objectively and is reported on your tax return. Net revenues could be more challenging because that number is relatively easy to manipulate. For example, you could decide you need to hire your cousin to do a big consulting job at the end of the year so that you can reduce your net revenues down to zero. On the other hand, using gross revenues as the basis of payment to investors is very risky because you will owe them the same amount regardless of what happens to your costs or expenses. The price of an input could double, and you would still owe the same amount.

2. What is the payoff amount? This is a multiple of the original investment amount.

3. Will there be a payment holiday, aka honeymoon period, up front? If so, how long will it be?

4. Will payments be monthly, quarterly, annually, or something else?

There is another model that also provides for variable payments based on company performance. But in this variation, the payments are made during a certain period of time and then they end on an agreed-on date. So, unlike the model discussed earlier in which the payoff amount is set and the time for payment is open ended, in this model, the time for payment is set and the payoff amount is open ended. The way this works is that the company promises to pay a certain percentage of free cash flow, gross revenues, gross margin, operating profit, or some other number every year (or some other shorter period) for a fixed number of years. At the end of that period, whatever the investor has received is the total payoff amount. The company may guarantee a certain minimum interest rate. This is recommended because otherwise, this instrument could look more like equity than debt and be recharacterized by the IRS as equity.

Another model is a combination of a fixed-interest-rate loan with "bonus" interest based on company performance. In this model, the base interest rate could be set at something like 2 percent. At the end of each fiscal year, the company could calculate an additional bonus interest payment based on some percentage of its free cash flow, gross revenues, gross margin, operating profit, or some other number.

In all three of these models, the investors may be more motivated than in a fixed-interest-rate scenario to do what they can to support the company's success because the company's success translates directly into higher payments for them.

What about Zero-Interest Loans?

So, you got really lucky and you have some investors who are willing to make you a loan with zero interest.

Depending on various factors, the IRS might treat your lenders as if they have received interest even though they haven't! There are some exceptions to this—for example, generally if the loan is for $10,000 or less. To avoid the lender's being taxed on interest she didn't receive, you may need to pay a minimum amount of interest. The IRS publishes a list of rates called *applicable federal rates* at https://apps.irs.gov/app/picklist/list/federalRates.html that are the minimum you need to charge to avoid this imputed interest issue.

What about Higher Interest Rates?

There is a legal concept called *usury* that caps the interest rate that can legally be charged by a lender. The maximum amount (usually 10–18% annual interest) and the details of when the cap applies vary by state. If you enter into a loan agreement with an investor that is not compliant with applicable usury law, the loan could be unenforceable, and there could be other negative consequences. Some investors are willing to take the risk, but more knowledgeable investors will likely want to avoid making a loan that is not consistent with applicable usury law.

Staggered Maturity

Instead of offering the same interest rate and maturity to all investors, you could offer options for investors to choose from. For example,

+ Five-year note at 3 percent interest
+ Six-year note at 3.5 percent interest
+ Seven-year note at 4 percent interest

This type of offering with staggered maturities (i.e., due dates) mitigates the challenge of having all of your promissory notes coming due at the same time.

Letting Investors Participate in a Big Payday

Let's say you decide to offer promissory notes to your potential investors. And let's say your company has the potential someday of getting very big and doing an IPO or being sold to a larger company at a high price. You have no idea whether this will happen, but it theoretically *could* happen. Investors in debt securities would not benefit from this kind of event because the amount they get paid pack is pretty much fixed regardless of what happens (and usually limited by usury law). Investors may feel that this is unfair.

In this kind of situation, you may want to offer your investors something in addition to the promissory note, known as an "equity kicker." This generally gives your investors the right to purchase equity in your company in the future at a pre-determined price. If your company doesn't have a big payday, no big deal; the equity kicker (usually called a *warrant*) just becomes a worthless piece of paper. If there is a big payday, the investor can get in on the deal by exercising the right to purchase equity at the pre-determined price, assuming that this price is lower than the market price at the time of exercise. Note that when you are offering warrants in conjunction with a note, you should charge a fee for the warrants to prevent possible negative tax consequences. (Consult with an attorney or tax professional for details.)

Examples

Now for some examples of creative debt offerings to give you a taste of the options that are available.

> Farm Fresh to You, a produce delivery business, has a Green Loan Program that offers a promissory note to its customers with a minimum investment of $2,000. The interest rate is tied to a market benchmark (one-year LIBOR rate). If you take your interest payment in the form of credits toward the organic produce that the company sells, your interest rate is 3 percent above the one-year LIBOR rate. If you choose to take your interest payment in the form of cash, the interest rate goes down to 1.5 percent above the one-year LIBOR rate. The company has raised millions of dollars from its customers with this offering.

> The Force for Good Fund is a program of a nonprofit 501(c)(3) that offers a promissory note to investors and then invests the funds raised into social enterprises that are unable to obtain conventional financing. The minimum investment is $1,000. The investors in the fund get an annual payment for eight years. The annual payment equals 95 percent of the returns from the investments made by the fund, distributed pro rata among the investors. Investors are not guaranteed any particular return, but the promissory note provides that if investors do not receive at least an average annual return of 2.5 percent by the end of the eight-year term, the fund will make a final payment out of its loss reserve

(consisting of charitable donations) to make up for the shortfall. The Force for Good Fund has raised over $800,000 as of this writing.

Red Bay Coffee, an Oakland-based coffee roaster and retailer, offered promissory notes which provide that the note holders will each receive his or her pro rata share of 5 percent of company gross revenues each year, beginning two years after the close of the offering. These payments will continue to be made until each note holder has received 1.5 times the original investment amount. Red Bay raised about $158,000 with this offering.

Options for Convertible Notes

A simple convertible note will contain the following basic provisions:

1. What is the term—that is, when does the note mature? This is usually eighteen months to five years. In Silicon Valley deals, it is rarely more than two years. This can be stressful because the pressure is on to raise equity before the end of the convertible note term.
2. What is the interest rate? This is usually simple interest calculated annually; it generally is not paid in cash to the investor, but accrued. Another thing to consider is whether you want accrued interest to automatically convert into equity or whether you would rather pay the interest back in cash when the conversion happens. If both the interest and principal convert, you will give up more equity than if just the principal converts.

3. What triggers a conversion of the note balance to equity? The trigger event is usually when the company raises equity investment at or above a certain amount. Raising that amount may automatically trigger the conversion of the convertible notes (both principal and possibly accrued interest) to equity or the conversion could be at the option of one or both of the parties. But you could have a different trigger if you don't plan to raise an equity round, as discussed in greater detail later.

4. What is the conversion discount? In exchange for the risk they take by investing early, the holders of convertible notes generally get a discount on the price of the equity they receive when their note converts. This is usually a 10–20 percent discount on the price that new investors (paying cash for the equity) pay.

5. What happens if the conversion trigger doesn't occur before the note term ends? This could mean that the principal and accrued interest become due and payable on the maturity date. However, some convertible notes either require or provide the option for the principal (and possibly the interest) to convert into common equity (i.e., the class of equity held by the founders) at a predetermined price. Note that if your convertible note contains a provision like that, it may not be considered debt from the IRS's standpoint because it doesn't have to be paid back. Also note that if the principal and interest are payable in cash when the term ends, it is very common for the company to ask the investors for an extension of time to raise an equity round. This is an uncomfortable position to be in because the investors are in the driver's

seat and may ask for more investor-friendly terms in
exchange for not demanding that you immediately pay
your debt to them.

6.   What happens if the company is sold during the term
of the note? There are various ways to handle this. It is
common to provide investors the option to be paid
back or to convert their notes into shares of the surviv-
ing entity.

There are a lot more variations that can be included in
a convertible note. For example, professional Silicon Valley
investors will often want a "valuation cap" included in the
note. This means that when the company raises equity, the
price paid for the equity by the convertible note holders is
the lower of (1) the discounted price discussed earlier (usually a 10–20% discount) and (2) the price they would pay if
the company was valued at the valuation cap at the time of
the conversion. This can result in a very big windfall to the
note holders if the equity investors agree to a valuation that
is much higher than the valuation cap.

You can also get creative with what triggers a conversion. For example, maybe you want your convertible notes
to be converted into equity if you achieve a certain milestone, such as a certain amount of revenues or the purchase
of a building. The conversion trigger could be automatic or
optional. If it is optional, it could be at the option of the
company, the investor, or both. If conversion is triggered by
anything other than a priced round—that is, the sale of
equity—you will have to determine how much equity the
note holders will be able to purchase with their note bal-

ances. This could be based on a valuation done at the time of the conversion trigger, or it could be based on a pre-determined price. The pre-determined price could be a set amount, or it could be an amount arrived at by doing some sort of calculation—for example, it could be some multiple of gross revenues from the most recently completed calendar year quarter.

Another term you can include is "most favored nation" status. This means that if you raise more money in the future in the form of convertible notes and the future investors get better terms than the current investors, the current investors have the right to switch to the more favorable note terms.

One caution about convertible notes: they inherently create uncertainty for your business. Because they are usually structured such that you have no idea at what price the notes will convert into equity and what the terms of the equity will be, you have to be careful. For example, let's say you sell $1 million in convertible notes with a 20 percent conversion discount. One year later, you raise $2 million in equity, which triggers a conversion of the notes. Your pre-money valuation was $2.5 million; you were hoping for a higher valuation, but that was the best you could negotiate. And to make the calculation easier, let's say you pay the interest to the convertible note holders in cash and only the principal converts. How much of your company do you own when all is said and done?

Assuming that before you raised equity, you owned 100 percent, after you raise equity, you now own only 43 percent—you have lost majority ownership of your baby!

How did this happen? Well, the value of the note holders' equity is $1.25 million because of their 20 percent discount, and the value of the equity investors' investment is $2 million. The pre-money valuation is $2.5 million. If you add in the additional $3.25 million in investment, the post-money valuation is $5.75 million and you own $2.5 million of that, which is 43 percent.

Also, because you don't know what the terms of the equity round will be, you don't know what rights your convertible note holders will have. It is possible they could end up with voting rights or other rights that you would rather they not have.

None of this means you shouldn't use convertible notes, but it does mean you should think through all of the possible consequences before you do.

Options for Equity

As creative as you can get with debt, equity offers even more possible variations. And, unlike with debt, with equity, the specifics will depend on the type of entity and how it is taxed.

Generally, there are two ways that equity investors can get compensated: (1) sharing in the company profits by receiving profit distributions or (2) selling their equity for a higher price than what they paid when they bought it (aka capital gain).

In the model used by venture capitalists, the investors make all their money using the second option. They buy stock for as low a price as they can get and, after several years, if the company is sold or goes public, the VCs make money by selling their stock at a much higher price than what they bought it for. They do not expect the company to pay profit distributions, because they want any profits to be plowed back in to pay for growth. Usually there aren't any profits anyway, because these companies are investing everything they have in growth.

Many people think that this is the only option for how equity investment can work. But this is not the case! If a company pays regular dividends, there may be no need to push for a sale of the company or an IPO. For example, Equal Exchange is a successful company that sells products like coffee and chocolate bars throughout the United States. Equal Exchange has raised tens of millions of dollars and has several hundred equity investors. The equity investors (preferred shareholders) receive an annual dividend at the discretion of the board, usually 5 percent. The investors are very happy to hold their investments for the long term because this is a very good return compared to the average that is paid by a bank certificate of deposit or stock market index fund.

We won't be able to cover every possible variation on the kinds of economic rights that can be offered to equity investors. We will cover the basics, and more resources for those who want to dig deeper are provided on the readers' resources website. (See the resources section of this book for how to access the site.)

Profit Distributions

One of the simplest ways to compensate equity investors is to give them a share of the profits. (Assuming you have profits—if you don't currently have profits, you can still offer a share of the future profits.) In a corporation, a payment to the shareholders is usually called a *dividend*, whereas in an LLC, it is usually called a *distribution*.

One nice thing you can offer to your equity investors is a *preference*. A preference means that the investors get their share of the profits before the founders. So, for example, you could say that until the equity investors get a 5 percent annual return on their investment (i.e., 5% of their initial investment amount), no profits will be paid to the founders. This doesn't mean that the founders won't be paid reasonable salaries. (Profits are calculated after the employees get their salaries and other expenses are accounted for.) This just means that they do not get to participate in the profits until after the investors have received some reasonable amount. If there is anything left over after that, then of course, the founders can take out some profit.

In a C Corp, if you decide to give your investors a preference to receive dividends first, you would create (in your articles of incorporation) a new class of stock called *preferred stock*. Preferred stock gives economic preferences to the shareholders who own it. Remember that an S Corp cannot have preferred stock because all shareholders must have the same economic rights. If you have an S Corp, it is usually very easy to switch to being taxed as a C Corp if you want to be able to offer preferred stock.

There is an infinite number of ways that preferred stock can be structured in terms of what rights the preferred shareholders have. This is something that can be negotiated with investors. Venture capitalists usually insist on receiving preferred stock with all kinds of economic and governance rights to protect their interests and ensure that they are well compensated if the company is sold or goes public. When you're dealing with other types of investors, you can generally keep things much simpler (and more balanced).

With an LLC, similar principles apply: you can create (in your operating agreement) a new class of membership called *preferred memberships* or *preferred units,* and the holders of these memberships or units would get some kind of preference to receive profit distributions.

Here are a couple of examples of terms of preferred equity:

> Our Harvest, a Cincinnati-based organic produce delivery service, created a class of nonvoting preferred stock with a targeted annual dividend of 5 percent. Common shareholders will only receive a profit distribution if the preferred shareholders receive the target dividend.

> Gather Restaurant in Berkeley, California, an LLC, offered to pay 95 percent of operating profits twice annually to preferred members on a pro rata basis until each investor receives the total amount of his or her initial investment in the form of profit distributions. Thereafter, preferred members will be paid 40 percent of operating profits pro rata. In addition, all preferred members receive an annual credit at the restaurant equal to 1 percent of the initial investment.

Cumulative versus Noncumulative Distributions

If a company offers *cumulative distributions,* it means that the equity investors earn a certain distribution every year no matter what. Companies can only pay distributions when they're solvent, so there may be some years when investors aren't paid anything. But if an investor has the right to cumulative distributions, the company is required to pay the amount of distributions earned each year at some point. For example, People's Community Market is a start-up grocery store in Oakland, California. When the company raised money, it did not have a location yet and did not expect to break even for a while. But the company offered preferred stock to their investors with a cumulative annual 3 percent dividend, meaning that every year, their investors accrue a 3 percent dividend. So if I invested in year 1 and the company didn't pay any dividends until year 7, the company would owe me 21 percent of my original investment in year 7 (3% per year times seven years), plus 3 percent per year for as long as I own the stock.

Most companies do not offer cumulative distributions, but it is a good option to keep in mind if you want to reassure your investors that they will earn a return every year, even when the company is not profitable.

A Note about Valuation

When selling equity, there may be a lot of fuss over the question of valuation. The reason why Silicon Valley–style investors are obsessed with the question of valuation is that they want to buy equity at the lowest possible price and then sell it later at a much higher price. When you hear them talking about a "30x return," this is what they mean. For every $1 they paid to buy the equity, they want to sell that same amount of equity for $30, ideally within five to seven years of their initial investment.

But if you are paying profit distributions to your investors, valuation may not matter very much. For example, let's say you sell $10,000 worth of preferred stock. Your offering documents state that $10,000 represents 1 percent of the total value of the company ($1 million). Every year, you pay a 6 percent dividend. Your investors are very happy with this return, because none of their other investments pay that much, plus they also get a nice discount on the company's products. Let's say that one day you realize that you made a mistake in your offering documents: the company is actually valued at $10 million, not $1 million. Your investors really only own .1 percent of the value of the company, not 1 percent as they had thought. Do your investors really care? No, because they still get the same annual dividend and a discount. You can see how in this scenario, the valuation really doesn't matter.

But what if the company is sold to a larger company? Then it would matter, right? That depends on the terms of your investment. We will dive into that question in the next section, when we discuss the question of investor exit.

Exit (aka Sale of Equity)

As we've discussed, the VC model of investing makes money via a sale of the investor's equity. This usually happens when there is a "liquidity event"—a sale of the company to another company or an IPO—that allows the investor to cash out. This is also known as an *exit*. The sale of the company or an IPO are just two of several ways that an investor can exit her equity investment.

What if you never plan to sell your company or do an IPO? That's okay; there are other ways for equity investors to be compensated. As discussed earlier, they can receive a share of the profits. But equity investors will also want to know how they will be able to eventually get their money back out (i.e., *exit*). So in the earlier example where investors are happily collecting a 6 percent dividend per year, what happens if an investor suddenly has a big medical bill and would really like to get her money back out? The investor has to sell her equity—that is, exit the investment. There are a few ways that she can do this. Maybe the company will be sold to another company or do an IPO. This is not an option for most companies, so this would be a long shot. Other options are (1) the investor sells her equity to someone else who wants to become an investor in the company, or (2) the company buys the equity back. This second option is called a *put* or a *redemption*. We'll discuss these options in greater detail later.

You want to think about options for exit before offering equity to investors. Too many companies sell equity to investors with absolutely no thought to what happens if the investors want to get their money back out. If you leave this undefined in your investor agreement, the situation can get very messy. Your investors could try to pressure you to sell the company when you don't want to, or they could demand that you buy their equity back and pay for an expensive third-party appraisal to determine the fair market value. You can avoid these kinds of headaches by thinking through how your equity investors will exit and spelling that out in the legal documents at the time they make their investment.

Sale of Equity to a Third Party

It is possible that your equity investors could exit their investment by selling their equity to someone else. This can be challenging because there is often no market for this kind of investment; unfortunately, there is no exchange for equity in private companies comparable to the New York Stock Exchange, which makes selling shares in public companies relatively easy.

There also can be legal limitations on the ability of your equity investors to sell to someone else. Your own organizing documents may contain limits on equity holders' rights to transfer their equity, and there may be limits imposed under state and/or federal securities law depending on what compliance strategy you used to sell the equity in the first place. (This is discussed in greater detail in step 4.)

Assuming there are no legal limitations on resale, you may be able to facilitate the process for your investors who are looking for a buyer for their equity. The company Real Goods Trading set up an online "bulletin board" to help sellers connect with buyers of their stock. It is very important to work with a knowledgeable securities lawyer before doing something like this, but it certainly can be done.

Redemption

Equal Exchange, the seller of fair trade coffee, chocolate, and other products we talked about earlier, designed a great system to make sure its equity investors could exit with minimal hassle or disruption to the company. As noted earlier, Equal Exchange pays an annual dividend that its investors are very happy with, so very few investors want to exit. But of course, from time to time, someone will want his or her money out for one reason or another. When this happens, the investor knows the rules because they are written into the investment documents. The investor can send in a request that the company buy back his or her stock. The price is set: it is the same price that the investor originally paid. Investors may not request a redemption for the first two years of investment. After that, if the investor requests a redemption in year 3, the company has the discretion to pay only 70 percent of the original amount invested. In year 4, the company can pay 80 percent. In year 5, the company can pay 90 percent. After that, the investor is entitled to request a redemption of his or her stock for the same amount that he or she originally paid. Even then, the company may refuse the redemption if it would impair the company's ability to operate effectively. The company may also choose to redeem the shares with a promissory note instead of cash, or a combination of a note and cash.

Equal Exchange also has the right to buy back (i.e., *call*) shares from its investors at its discretion (also at the same price that the investor originally paid).

This is one way to handle the question of how your investors will get their money back out.

Another structure involves periodic mandatory redemptions of the equity. The redemptions can be tied to the cash flow of the company, such that the better the cash flow, the more shares the company will buy back from the investor in that period. For example, the total redemption value of the shares could be 2.5 times the original investment. The funds to be used for redemption purposes would be defined as X percent of the company's cash flow. Each period, the company would use that percentage of cash flow to buy back stock until all of the stock is redeemed at the pre-determined price (i.e., 2.5 times the original investment).[31]

Another structure provides the investor the right to "put" its equity back to the company at a pre-determined price. For example, the investor could invest $100,000 in company equity and be given the right to sell the equity back to the company for $150,000 five years after the investment was made.

These kinds of redemption models in which you plan in advance how your investors will exit instead of leaving it open ended are sometimes called *structured exits*.

Sale of the Company

It's a good idea to include provisions in your investor agreement about what happens in case you do sell the company.

It is very common to provide investors with a *liquidation preference*. This means that if the company is sold (or goes out of business), the investors get first dibs on getting paid, up to a certain amount. There are many ways to structure a liquidation preference. The simplest is to say that the preferred equity investors get paid back their original investment before the common equity holders (i.e., the founders) get any money out. If there is anything left over after that, it can be split pro rata among all of the equity investors or just the common equity holders. Here is an example of how this would work. Let's say you raise $500,000 from preferred investors and they own 25 percent of your company (this means that your post-money valuation is $2 million). Three years later, you sell the company for $10 million. Your preferred investors would get $500,000 (their original investment) right off the top. The remaining $9.5 million could be shared pro rata among all of you. So you would get 75 percent of the $9.5 million ($7.125 million), and they would get 25 percent of the $9.5 million ($2.375 million). Thus they would end up with $2.875 million total. Not a bad return on a $500,000 investment!

A liquidation preference usually kicks in as well if the company goes out of business. This means that if things don't work out, your preferred equity investors can at least be assured that they will have first dibs on anything left over after the creditors are paid off. If there is not enough left to pay all the equity investors their original investment amounts, they share on a pro rata basis in whatever is left.

Other Economic Rights That Can Be Offered to Equity Investors

When you are working with a sophisticated professional investor, the provisions he or she might request are too numerous to cover in detail here and generally won't even come up unless you are dealing with a Silicon Valley–style raise, in which case you would probably be reading a different book! I'll just mention a few of them here, but I suggest that you not worry about the more exotic provisions that can be included in preferred equity. Most investors will be very satisfied with a simple arrangement in which they receive preferred profit distribution and first dibs on getting their money back in the case of a liquidation.

Note that sophisticated professional equity investors in a Silicon Valley–style raise will almost always be investing in a Delaware corporation taxed under Subchapter C. The provisions listed here are generally found in investments in corporate stock, but could also be included in an LLC equity investment.

Conversion rights. This is the right to convert preferred shares to common shares, usually on a one-for-one basis. This can come into play if the company is sold at a valuation that is much higher than the price at which the shares were originally purchased or if the company goes public. If the preferred stock has a capped liquidation preference, converting into common shares can result in a much higher payout to the investor.

Anti-dilution protection. This is a provision that protects the preferred equity holders in the case of a second sale of equity at a lower valuation. It does this by adjusting the rate at which preferred equity converts into common equity.

Preemptive rights. This is the right of equity investors to purchase equity in future equity raises, so as to maintain their ownership percentage.

Right of first refusal and co-sale rights. These come into play if the founders ever try to sell their shares. The investors have a right of first refusal to purchase the founder shares or, if they don't want to purchase the founder shares, to sell their own shares to whoever purchases the founder shares.

Registration rights. These are rights to require the company to conduct a federally registered public offering.

Economic Rights That Can Be Offered to Both Equity and Debt Investors

You may want to provide protections to your investors to help them feel more comfortable about investing. For example, let's say you offer a promissory note that is interest only for several years, and the principal is due in one big payment at maturity. This could make your investors nervous: What if you can't afford to make that big payment at maturity? You could commit to regularly set aside funds in a special account, called a *sinking fund*, so that you have enough to pay back your note holders when the notes become due. The following are some additional rights you could offer to your investors:

Pledge regarding liens on the company's property. This is a promise not to enter into financing arrangements that would result in liens on the company's property.

Pledge regarding other obligations. This is a promise not to incur any additional debt (or any additional debt in excess of a certain amount or that is not subordinated to the rights of the current investors) until the current investors have been paid.

Pledge regarding profit distributions to company principals. This is a promise not to pay any profit distributions to the company principals until the investors have been paid. Of course, this does not prevent payment of reasonable salaries.

Vesting of founders' shares. This is a provision that incentivizes the founders to stay at the company by preventing their stock from being fully owned by them unless they stay with the company for a period of time. This is not a direct benefit to the investors, but some will appreciate it because it gives them assurance that the people they chose to invest in will be likely to stay on at the company for a while.

Security interest for debt investors. It is possible to secure a loan with collateral, such as business equipment. This means that if you are unable to pay your investors, they can take title to the collateral. This takes some paperwork and can be a hassle if you have multiple investors.

Information rights. These are rights of investors to receive certain information about the company (e.g., an annual financial report). Equity investors generally have statutory rights to receive certain information. You can offer additional rights if you choose, and you can offer information rights to debt investors.

Your Decision

What economic rights would you like to offer your investors? Make sure they are consistent with your expectations and plans for your business so that you can comfortably fulfill your promises!

DECISION POINT 4: GOVERNANCE RIGHTS

The next question, after you decide on the economic rights you'll offer to investors, is whether your investors will have any decision-making authority with respect to your business.

Decision-Making Rights in Debt Instruments

Debt investors typically do not have decision-making rights with respect to the company they are investing in. However, you could give them rights to approve certain company actions, and, in any case, they will likely have rights with respect to the investment itself. For example, in Silicon Valley–style convertible note raises, there are often provisions in the convertible note that require the approval of a majority of the note holders (by amount of money invested) before certain things can happen, such as amendment of the convertible note or prepayment of the note.

Decision-Making Rights in Equity Instruments

It is not uncommon for holders of equity to have some voting rights. The company founders usually own common stock (in a corporation) or something similar to common stock (in an LLC). Each share of common stock usually comes with one vote. In LLCs, the founding members usually have the right to vote in proportion to their ownership stake in the LLC.

What does it mean to have voting rights? It doesn't mean that the investor gets to weigh in on every single decision that the company makes. The primary voting right is the right to elect the board of directors (in a corporation) or manager (in an LLC), which has the ultimate governance authority over the company.

So the people who start the company will hold equity that gives them voting rights. Then the question is, do the people who bring money to the table—the investors—also get voting rights? If so, what exactly will those voting rights be? Depending on state law, equity investors are generally not required to have voting rights with respect to most issues. However, some equity investors will want some level of control in exchange for their investment. This is generally negotiable. If you don't want to give up control, you can choose investors who are happy to be passive. This is what Equal Exchange does. Its investors have essentially no voting rights.

Venture capitalists generally want *a lot* of control. They usually will require you to give them the following:

+ Right to vote on the same basis as the common shareholders
+ Right to appoint one or more board members
+ Protective provisions—special approval rights with respect to matters of particular significance, such as new financings, payment of distributions, charter or bylaw amendments that affect the rights of investors, liquidation, merger, and so on
+ The requirement to include a director chosen by the investors in all board committees
+ The requirement that the board meet a minimum of once per month
+ Access to company facilities, personnel, and information

This is why so many founders who raise money from venture capitalists shake in their boots every month before their board meeting.

Between the two extremes of not giving away any voting rights at all and pretty much giving up control of the company, as happens in a venture deal, there are many options in between. Here are a few to consider:

+ The equity investors get voting rights on the same basis as the founders (usually voting in proportion to ownership percentage).
+ Each equity investor gets one vote regardless of the percentage of ownership.
+ The investors get to vote as a class and choose one or some other number of directors/managers (usually less than a majority).
+ The investors generally don't have any voting rights, but they get veto power over certain major decisions, such as the sale or merger of the company.
+ The investors have no voting rights unless the company fails to comply with a certain obligation, such as the payment of some minimum annual distribution.

Your Decision

Decide what decision-making authority, if any, you want your investors to have.

DECISION POINT 5: ADD THE PERKS

Great! Now you know the economic rights and voting rights that you want to offer your investors. Don't forget to add in some perks! These can include an investors-only discount, a special seat at your restaurant, a bottomless mug of coffee at your café, their name on your wall, investors-only events, and the like. Get creative! Don't underestimate how valuable it is for your investors to feel that they are part of a like-minded community and to be able to tell their friends that they invested in a cool company. Do a little market research when talking to potential investors to get a sense of what they would value. Sometimes they value the perks more than the financial returns. The economic theories about rational actors making purely economic decisions have been proven false by countless experiments (for example, check out the work of Nobel Prize winners Danny Kahneman and Amos Tversky). People make decisions based on numerous factors in addition to pure economic considerations. Get creative and give your ideal investors what they want!

Be sure to check with a knowledgeable tax specialist about how your perks might affect you and your investors from a tax perspective.

Your Decision

Make a list of perks to offer to your investors. You can use perks as a way to encourage larger investments by providing certain perks only to investors who invest above a certain amount.

MAKING IT LEGAL

Now that you know what you want to offer, you will probably need to get a lawyer to put it into the proper legal form. If you tell the lawyer what you want and the lawyer looks at you like you're crazy and tries to persuade you to use something more standard, run—don't walk—out of that lawyer's office! You need to find a lawyer who is willing to work with you to put your wishes onto paper. Of course, you may dream up something that is not legally possible or is so complicated that it will cost a fortune to document. You need to find a lawyer who is excited to support you in your creativity, but also knowledgeable enough to tell you when you need to make a few tweaks.

The assessments section at the back of the book has a Capital Raising Decision Tool you can use to think through the decision about what to offer to investors.

choose your legal compliance strategy

In chapter 3 of part 1, I provided an overview of the legal requirements for offering investment opportunities (i.e., securities law). Let's quickly recap that overview so we can dive into the details of the options that are available.

A *security* is any arrangement that allows the contributor of funds to receive a financial return on his or her investment, usually in the form of interest or a share of profits or an appreciation in the value of the investment. All of the investment instruments discussed in step 3 are securities.

No matter how creative you get with what you're offering to investors, chances are it will be covered by securities law.

You need a securities compliance strategy for both federal law *and* for the laws of any states where you want to offer your investment opportunity.

The general rule is that before you make an offering of securities, you must register the offering with both the federal government—the Securities and Exchange Commission

(SEC)—and with the securities regulators of every state where you will be offering the investment opportunity.

Registration, especially at the federal level, can be an expensive and time-consuming process, so it is very helpful if you can find an exemption to the registration requirements that applies to your situation.

As we discussed in chapter 3, answering the following questions will help you choose your legal compliance strategy:

+ Do you want to be able to publicly advertise your securities offering?
+ Do you want to be able to include both accredited and unaccredited investors, or do you want to limit your offering to accredited investors only? Also, if you want to include unaccredited investors, how many would you like to be able to have?
+ How much do you want to raise?
+ In what states do you want to offer your securities? Just one? A few? All of them?

Generally, legal compliance is cheaper and easier when

+ You do not publicly advertise the offering.
+ You offer the opportunity only to accredited investors.
+ You are raising $5 million or less.
+ Your potential investors are all in one state.

This is because the securities laws assume that public advertising can create more potential hazards for unsophisticated investors, that accredited investors need less protection, and that larger raises can cause more harm if things don't work out. And, of course, more states can often mean more compliance hurdles.

However, there are ways to publicly advertise the offering, include both accredited and unaccredited investors, raise more than $5 million, and raise from residents of multiple states. So don't feel the need to take the cheapest and easiest path if it won't allow you to reach your ideal investors and raise money in the way that fits best with your unique situation.

The next section will discuss options for private offerings. Then we will discuss options for public offerings. Finally, we will talk about special considerations for nonprofits and cooperatives.

PRIVATE OFFERINGS

A **private offering,** or **private placement,** is one in which there is no public advertising. You don't announce at a public event that you're raising money. You don't post about your offering on social media. You don't invite a bunch of people to a workshop or webinar where you ask them to invest. The only way you communicate with potential investors is privately, which means one-on-one via telephone or in person or possibly by e-mail. (E-mail is not ideal because it can be so easily forwarded to others and become more like a mass communication.)

Private offerings can be challenging because you have to identify specific potential investors and reach out to them one-on-one. Some entrepreneurs may say "I don't know any investors!" and assume that they cannot raise money using a private offering. However, if you are willing to talk to a lot of people and possibly end up with a larger number of smaller investors, you may find that a private offering can work for you.

The following sections describe the various compliance strategies you can use for a private offering.

Rule 506(b)—Accredited Investors Only

Rule 506(b) is a federal rule that allows you to avoid registering your offering if you only include accredited investors. (Actually, you are technically allowed to include a limited number of unaccredited investors, but the disclosure requirements are so onerous that it is usually not worth the extra expense and effort.) This is the rule that is used for Silicon Valley–style deals with angels and VCs. It's not enough to make sure that all of the investors are accredited; you need to not even make an investment *offering* to an unaccredited investor. This is why businesses using this rule ask potential investors to complete a questionnaire to ensure that they are accredited before even discussing the investment opportunity.

The nice thing about Rule 506(b) is that it preempts the states from imposing their own substantive requirements when you make an offering to their residents. However, the states *are* allowed to require notice filings and fees. Thus if you use Rule 506(b) and you have investors in ten different states, you will need to ensure that you do all the required filings in those states. You also have to file federal **Form D** (described in more detail in the glossary). These filings are usually due within fifteen days after your first sale.

Rule 504—Up to $5 Million

Let's say you decide you don't want to use Rule 506(b) because you want to be able to include unaccredited investors. Rule 504 may be the right choice for you.

Rule 504 does not impose any limits on the number of unaccredited investors to whom you can offer or sell your investment opportunity. However, unlike with Rule 506(b), there is no preemption of state law. So you have to be very careful about making sure you comply with the laws of the state where your business is located and each state where you plan to talk to potential investors. In some states, such as New York and Wisconsin, you have to file a form and pay a fee *before* you can talk to any investors in those states. Each state has its own interesting quirks. Many limit the number of investors you can have from that state or the number of unaccredited investors. California, for example, allows an unlimited number of accredited investors and up to thirty-five unaccredited investors, and requires that all unaccredited investors have a substantial preexisting relationship with the company and its principals or meet certain sophistication requirements. Some states require filings and fees; others don't.

Even though Rule 506(b) limits what the states can require and Rule 504 doesn't, in practice this distinction may not make a big difference for you, depending on where your investors are located. In fact, the required filings under Rule 506(b) can sometimes be more expensive and onerous than what is required under Rule 504. The big difference is that with Rule 504, states can be as quirky and demanding as they want to be because they are not preempted from imposing substantive requirements. For example, let's say you have a potential investor in New York. If you're doing your offering under Rule 504 and you accidentally accept an investment from a New York resident before doing your New York filing, there is nothing you can do to make the investment from the New York resident legal. By contrast, if you're doing your offering under Rule 506(b), the state is not allowed to make your life so difficult. Yes, it will still require a filing and a fee, but they can be submitted *after* you have brought on your New York investor.

You can raise up to $5 million per year under Rule 504, and you have to file a federal Form D.

Intrastate Exemption—One State Only

If you want to raise money in only one state and it's the same state where you have your principal place of business, you can use the federal intrastate exemption. (This exemption for intrastate offerings was recently updated by the SEC to make it easier to use—the new and improved rule is called Rule 147A.) The nice thing about the intrastate exemption is that there is no limit on how much you can raise, and there is no federal filing required. There is also no limit on the number of unaccredited investors you can include. However, as in Rule 504, there is no preemption of state law. You must therefore make sure you comply with the securities laws of the state where you're making your offering (which may impose filing requirements, limits on the number of investors, caps on the amounts that can be raised, and so on). As already noted, each state is different and can be quite quirky.

Other Federal Exemptions for Private Offerings

In addition to the exemption discussed in this section, there are also exemptions from the federal registration requirement for nonprofit organizations and agricultural cooperatives, discussed in more detail later.

Section 4(a)(2) of the 1933 Securities Act exempts private offerings from the registration requirement. Because this provision is rather vague, it can be difficult to know whether you qualify to use it. Case law interpreting this section mandates that for this exemption to apply, the purchasers of securities must have access to detailed information about the business similar to what an insider would have. As the number of purchasers increases and their relationship to the company and its management becomes more remote, it is more difficult to show that the offering qualifies for this exemption. Rule 506(b) is actually a safe harbor for compliance with Section 4(a)(2). A **safe harbor** is a list of requirements that, if you meet them, you are guaranteed to be in compliance with the statute. If you don't meet the safe harbor requirements, you may still be in compliance with the statute, but you will have less certainty about it. To be on the safe side, most issuers use the safe harbor (Rule 506(b)) rather than relying on Section 4(a)(2). However, for securities offerings made to insiders like cofounders, it's generally fine to simply rely on Section 4(a)(2).

PUBLIC OFFERINGS

Let's say you really want to be able to shout from the rooftops that you are offering an investment opportunity. If that's the case, a **public offering** is the way to go! With one exception (offerings under the federal crowdfunding exemption), which I will discuss in more detail in a later section, there are no limits on how you can advertise a public offering of securities as long as you comply with all the requirements of your chosen compliance strategy.

I want to clarify something here: doing a public offering of securities is not the same thing as "going public." Going public means becoming a public reporting company under the 1934 Securities Exchange Act. You can do a public offering without becoming a public company.

A great thing about public offerings (except under Rule 506(c), discussed in the next section) is that you can have almost an unlimited number of both accredited and unaccredited investors. This is in contrast to private offerings, in which you are likely to be limited to somewhere between ten and thirty-five unaccredited investors, depending on which states your investors are in and which private offering compliance strategy you're using.

How Many Investors Can You Have in a Public Offering?

With a public offering, the only limit on the number of investors you can have comes from a federal law, which requires that a company with (1) more than five hundred unaccredited or two thousand total holders of a class of equity securities *and* (2) at least $10 million in assets is required to become a public reporting company. Most companies will want to avoid "going public," as the cost of being a public company is quite high. Note that investors in a federal crowdfunding offering (discussed later) don't count toward the five hundred or two thousand investor caps (assuming you are current on the ongoing annual reporting required under the federal crowdfunding regulations, have total assets of $25 million or less, and have engaged the services of a transfer agent).

Being able to both publicly advertise your offering *and* have a virtually unlimited number of both accredited and unaccredited investors is a major advantage of public offerings. The compliance time and effort can be greater than for a private offering, but the trade-off may well be worth it.

Before we dive into the compliance options for public offerings, I would like to provide some history of how the number of public offering options has expanded in the last few years.

In 2009, I met attorney Janelle Orsi. We both loved working with creative, innovative, entrepreneurial change makers, and we hated to see them getting stymied by complicated legal requirements that were hard for them to understand and comply with. We decided to start a nonprofit organization called Sustainable Economies Law Center to address this problem with legal education and advocacy.

We invited law students to volunteer with us during the summer of 2010. One of the issues we tackled that summer was the securities laws. We learned that the SEC has a process that allows citizens to submit petitions requesting rule changes. That summer, our student interns drafted a petition requesting an exemption from registration requirements for public securities offerings in which the maximum that any single person could invest was $100. Although the SEC did not respond to the petition, it began to get attention: hundreds of letters of support were submitted to the SEC, and a member of the White House staff publicly expressed support. Before we knew it, President Obama was proposing a federal **investment crowdfunding** exemption, and Congress was holding hearings on the topic. On November 23, 2011, an investment crowdfunding law passed the House of Representatives by a vote of 345 to 10. The Senate made some changes, and the JOBS (Jumpstart Our Business Startups) Act was signed by President Obama on April 5, 2012. I was there at the signing ceremony in the Rose Garden!

The law had changed quite a bit from what we had originally proposed. The per-investor cap is much higher than $100! In addition to the crowdfunding section, the JOBS Act includes several other sections (known as titles) that address various aspects of securities law. Title III is the section that creates an investment crowdfunding exemption. The JOBS Act also created two other new tools for making public offerings of securities (Rule 506(c) and Regulation A+), discussed later.

One important thing to remember is that it was possible to do public securities offerings before the JOBS Act. However, before the JOBS Act went into effect, there was no practical way to do a public securities offering that was open to residents of all fifty states (it's actually fifty-four jurisdictions—the fifty states plus the District of Columbia, Guam, Puerto Rico, and the US Virgin Islands). Before the JOBS Act, you could do a public offering of securities in one or a few states, but to do it in all fifty states would have been prohibitively expensive and onerous. (There is an exception to this for agricultural co-ops, discussed later.)

step 4: choose your legal compliance strategy

Rule 506(c)—Accredited Investors Only

Rule 506(c) was created under the JOBS Act (Title II). It went into effect in the fall of 2013. It allows unlimited public advertising of the securities offering and has the same preemption of state law as Rule 506(b). All investors must be accredited, and there is a greater burden on the company than under Rule 506(b) to ensure that all investors are accredited. (Under Rule 506(b), the practice is to have investors answer a questionnaire about their income and net worth, whereas under Rule 506(c), it is recommended that you obtain proof of accredited status.)

Rule 506(c) has not proven to be very popular. Some websites have sprung up where you can list a 506(c) offering, but according to SEC data, fewer than 20 percent of offerings under 506(c) reach their goal, and the average raised is only $210,000. My guess as to why 506(c) has not resulted in a great deal of successful raises is that when you are limited to accredited investors, your potential pool is so small that being able to publicly advertise does not greatly increase your ability to reach investors. Also, some accredited investors are turned off by having to submit proof of their accredited status before being able to invest in an offering made under 506(c).

Rule 504—Up to $5 Million

Remember that you can use Rule 504 for a private offering, as discussed earlier? You can also use it for a public offering!

The way this works is that Rule 504 allows public advertising as long as you register the offering in every state where you want to be able to accept investors. (Or, if there is no registration required in the state where you want to

127

make the offering, you register in at least one state that *does* require registration and then deliver the disclosure document you created for the registration process in that state to *all* potential investors.)

For example, let's say you want to publicly offer an investment opportunity in Massachusetts and Vermont. Under Rule 504, you can do that, as long as you don't raise more than $5 million in any twelve-month period. However, you first have to register the offering under state law. So you submit some materials to the Massachusetts securities regulators, including a *prospectus* (aka disclosure document or offering circular) (see the readers' resources website for examples of prospectuses), some forms, and a filing fee. The Massachusetts regulators review the materials and may have some questions or requests for further information. Eventually, they give you the go-ahead to publicly offer your investment opportunity in Massachusetts. You submit similar materials to the regulators in Vermont, and they give you the go-ahead as well. This process can take anywhere from one to five months depending on the state. Some states are much more challenging than others. For example, some states require that a CPA review or audit your financial statements, which can cost thousands of dollars. Other states are very strict about what kinds of offerings they will allow. For example, if you want to offer a debt security in Pennsylvania, you will need to provide evidence that you have the capacity to meet your obligations to your investors.

Recall that we talked about the fact that federal registration is extremely onerous and expensive. This is not necessarily true for state-level registration. Many states have a relatively simple and pain-free registration process. Yes, it can take some time and effort, but the regulators are there to guide you. There is another benefit of going through the state registration process. The state regulators have lots of experience with securities offerings. They know what kinds of information are generally a good idea to discuss and disclose in a prospectus. If they have concerns about your prospectus, they will let you know and ask you to make changes. Although this can be a bit of a hassle sometimes, the end result is a prospectus that you can be fairly confident meets professional standards for the kinds of disclosures that should be made to potential investors. If things don't go as planned and you end up with disgruntled investors who are looking for a basis for a lawsuit, they are much less likely to be successful if your prospectus has gone through this review process with state securities regulators.

Intrastate Exemption—One State Only

As with Rule 504, you can do a public offering under the intrastate exemption as you can a private offering, as long as you comply with state law. So if your business is in California and you want to raise money from California investors using a public offering, you can use the intrastate exemption, and there is no cap on the amount you can raise. You just need to register the offering with the California securities regulators.

In some states, it is even easier than that. After the JOBS Act was signed into law in 2012, several years went by, and federal investment crowdfunding was still not legal because the SEC had to complete the rule-making process.

Many states got impatient and passed state-level investment crowdfunding laws that provide an exemption from the full state registration process for offerings that meet certain requirements (usually an annual cap on the amount that can be raised and a per-investor cap). These laws greatly reduce the time and effort required for conducting public offerings within these states. The laws vary a great deal from state to state. (See the readers' resources website for a list of links to state investment crowdfunding laws.)

Many of the state crowdfunding laws can only be used in conjunction with the federal intrastate exemption, but others can be used in conjunction with Rule 504, which means that you could use a state crowdfunding exemption in one state and also offer your investment opportunity in other states at the same time (as long as you comply with the laws of those states).

A Note about the SCOR (Small Company Offering Registration) Form

The North American Securities Administrators Association (NASAA), the association of state securities regulators, has made some efforts to standardize securities compliance requirements from state to state. Decades ago, NASAA created a form called SCOR (also known as U-7). The SCOR form was designed to be a generic form that would be accepted by all states to register a public offering. The idea was that you could fill out just one form and submit it to multiple states to register your offering. Unfortunately, the states are too ornery to comply with standardized requirements, so use of the SCOR form may work well in some states and not in others. To make matters worse, the form itself is not fun to fill out, in my opinion. If you decide to register a public offering in one or more states, you should do some research about whether the SCOR form is advisable to use in those states.

If you do use the SCOR form, you may be able to use what's known as *regional coordinated review*. The idea of coordinated review is that you only have to work with one or two of the states—the lead jurisdictions—which will coordinate review and comments from all states within the region in which you want to offer your securities. Yes, you still have to respond to comments and questions from *all* of the states!

A Note about Impound Accounts

When registering a public offering at the state level, you should be prepared for the regulators to require you to set up an *impound*. This means that investment funds must be held by a bank in an escrow account until a predetermined minimum has been raised. If you aren't able to raise the minimum within a specified period, all the money is returned to the investors. If you do raise the minimum within the specified period, the funds are released from the impound. Some states feel that this is very important for investor protection and impose the requirement on pretty much all offerings; others require it only if you are raising capital for a specific purpose and need a minimum amount of capital to move forward (e.g., purchase of a large piece of equipment).

Title III of the JOBS Act—the Federal Crowdfunding Exemption

As you can see from the discussion of the other options for public offerings (which have been legal for decades), until the JOBS Act, there was no easy way to make an offering in all fifty states because you had to ensure compliance with the laws of each state in which you were making an offering.

The federal crowdfunding exemption (also known as *regulation crowdfunding*) created a new option that preempts the states from requiring any state-level compliance, with one exception: states may require a filing for companies using the federal crowdfunding exemption if that company is based in that state or raises a majority of its investments in that state. As of this writing, only two states have adopted state-level filing requirements.

The JOBS Act is revolutionary because all of a sudden, you can offer your investment opportunity to anyone in the United States!

There are some trade-offs that come with using the federal investment crowdfunding exemption that you do need to consider when deciding whether it is right for you.

First, you can only raise up to $1 million per year (this number is increased regularly to keep up with inflation—as of this writing it has been increased to $1,070,000).

Second, you are required to use an intermediary web-based portal that has registered with the SEC and FINRA (the Financial Industry Regulatory Authority). Here is a list of the intermediaries that you can choose from: www .finra.org/about/funding-portals-we-regulate

Note that there may be some licensed broker-dealers who are not on this list who also offer Title III intermediary services.

Although in some ways it is nice to be able to use a third-party platform to make your offering (the investing process is managed by the platform; it may publicize your offering to its community; investors sometimes feel more comfortable investing through an intermediary; etc.), the downside is that the platform will take fees, and there are limits on what you are allowed to say about the offering outside of the platform, as discussed further later.

Unlike with state-level registrations, with Title III you are not required to submit a prospectus that will be reviewed and commented on by any regulatory authority. The onus is on you to make sure that you provide high-quality information to your potential investors. Although this makes the process of raising money under Title III much quicker, cheaper, and easier than a state-level registration, it also leaves more room for investors to complain later that they did not receive adequate information to make an informed investment decision. Be sure to take the time to describe your business and your offering in detail. All that the crowdfunding regulations require is "a description of the business of the issuer and the anticipated business plan of the issuer." It's up to you to decide how you will fulfill this requirement. For a more complete list of the requirements for offering an investment opportunity under Title III, see the readers' resources website.

Per-Investor Cap

Under Title III, everyone (whether accredited or not) is limited in the total amount he or she can invest per year. The following are the per-investor caps (note that these numbers are adjusted regularly for inflation):

1. If either the investor's annual income or net worth is less than $100,000, then the cap is the greater of $2,000 or 5 percent of the lesser of the investor's annual income or net worth.
2. If both the investor's annual income and net worth are equal to or more than $100,000, then the cap is

10 percent of the lesser of the investor's annual income or net worth, not to exceed $100,000.

You can rely on the efforts of the crowdfunding intermediary to ensure that the aggregate amount of securities purchased by an investor will not cause the investor to exceed the limits. However, if you happen to know that the investor has exceeded the limits, you can't feign ignorance!

Requirements for Financial Statements

When you conduct your offering under Title III, you have to provide financial statements. If you're raising $100,000 or less, you have to provide company tax returns. You also have to provide financials that are prepared in accordance with generally accepted accounting principles (GAAP). If you're raising more than $100,000, you have to provide financials reviewed by a CPA. (These amounts are adjusted regularly for inflation.) After the first time you raise money under Title III, you have to provide audited financials if you're raising more than $500,000. The preparation of these statements can cost several thousand dollars.

Limitations on Communications

One of the premises of the federal investment crowdfunding exemption is that if communication occurs only on the platform, it will be easier to ensure that the rules are being followed. Because of that, unlike for other kinds of public offerings, what you can say outside of the crowdfunding platform is very limited. The rules are a bit confusing, but to be on the safe side, the best thing to do is to tell everyone that you are offering an investment opportunity under Title III of the JOBS Act, aka the federal investment crowd-funding exemption, and if they want more information, they should go to your page on the platform.

The general rule is that you may not say anything about the offering outside of the platform. However, you are allowed to provide a public notice that includes no more than the following information:

+ A link to your fundraising page on the crowdfunding platform
+ A statement that you are conducting an offering under Section 4(a)(6) of the Securities Act (Title III of the JOBS Act)
+ The terms of the offering, which means
  + The amount of securities offered (i.e., how much you're raising)
  + The nature of the securities (i.e., equity versus debt and details about the economic and governance rights of the investors)
  + The price of the securities
  + The closing date of the offering period
+ The name of the issuer; the address, phone number, and website of the issuer; the e-mail address of a representative of the issuer; and a brief description of the business of the issuer

Please note that if you do not say anything about the terms of the offering (how much you're raising, the nature of the securities, the price of the securities, and the closing date of the offering), you're allowed to say whatever you want. (I discuss this in more detail at the end of this section.)

Minimum Raise and Time to Raise

You are required to set a minimum raise amount, and you will not be able to collect any funds unless you reach that minimum. Intermediaries usually let issuers decide how long they want to keep their offerings open.

Investors can pull out at the last minute. Under the law, investors have the right to change their mind about their investment up until two days before the end of the offering.

Ongoing Reporting

After raising money under Title III, you are required to file an annual report (including financial information prepared in accordance with GAAP), which you must post on your website. Thus your financials will be available for anyone to see, potentially for many years to come.

You must continue to file and publicly post annual reports until one of the following occurs:

+ You become a public reporting company.
+ You have filed at least one annual report and have fewer than three hundred security holders of record.
+ You have filed annual reports for at least three years and have total assets that do not exceed $10,000,000.
+ You or another party has repurchased all of the securities issued under Title III.
+ You liquidate or dissolve the business.

Details on What You Can Say during Your Title III Crowdfunding Campaign

One way to think about this is that every time you are getting ready to publicly advertise the offering, you have to decide whether or not you want to talk about the "terms" of the offering. As defined in the regulations, the terms are

- The amount of securities offered (i.e., how much you're raising)
- The nature of the securities (i.e., equity versus debt and details about the economic and governance rights of the investors)
- The price of the securities
- The closing date of the offering period

If you want to talk about the terms in your public advertising, you are very limited in what you can say—you can't go on and on about how great your company is, how it's better than the competition, and so on. If you don't feel the need to mention the terms, you can say whatever you want and just direct people to the intermediary for detailed information about the terms of the offering.

So, basically, there are two types of allowable communications outside of the platform (you can say whatever you want on the platform):

TYPE 1: NON-TERMS COMMUNICATION

Non-terms communication means that you can talk about the offering however you want as long as you don't mention the terms (as defined in the regulations).

This means you can do any kind of advertising in which you say you are doing an offering (although not *what* you are offering; that would be a "term") and include all sorts of information about the company, its track record, its mission, what it will use the money for, and the like. Of course, you can link to your fundraising page on the crowdfunding platform.

Whether you are identifying a term of the offering can be pretty subtle. "We are making an offering so that all our fans can be co-owners" might indirectly include a term because it's hinting that you are offering equity. Try to avoid hints as to what you are offering, and just send investors to the intermediary's site to find out more.

TYPE 2: COMMUNICATION THAT INCLUDES THE TERMS (AKA TOMBSTONE ADVERTISEMENT)

If you want to talk about the terms, you have to limit what you say to the short list of permitted items (the terms, the issuer's name and contact information, a brief description of the business, a statement that you're conducting the offering pursuant to Section 4(a)(6) of the Securities Act, and a link to your page on the platform).

"Brief description of the business of the issuer" means that you should not say more than just a general description of your principal products and services.

An advertisement that includes terms should not be connected to other communications because that will likely mean that you are including more information than is permissible. For example, if on your website you have a notice that includes terms and your website also has all kinds of detailed information about your company, the website considered as a whole will have way too much information to be counted as a tombstone ad.

A tombstone ad should not contain any links other than the link to your crowdfunding page. This is called a tombstone ad because it is so short: about what could fit on a tombstone.

Here is some useful information from CrowdCheck about talking to the media:

> Interviews with the media can be thorny because participation with a journalist makes the resulting article a communication of the company. In fact, the SEC Staff have stated that they don't see how interviews can easily be conducted, because even if the company personnel stick to the tombstone information (which would make for a pretty weird interview), the journalist could add non-tombstone information later, which would result in the article being a notice that didn't comply with the tombstone rule.
>
> The same thing could happen with interviews where the company tries to keep the interview on a non-terms basis. The

company personnel could refrain from mentioning any terms (again, it's going to be pretty odd saying, "Yes, we are making an offering of securities but I can't say what we are offering"), but the first thing the journalist is going to do is get the detailed terms from the company's campaign page on the platform's site, and again the result is that the article becomes a non-complying notice.

These rules apply to all articles that the company "participates in." This means that if you (or your publicists) tell the press, "Hey, take a look at the Company X crowdfunding campaign" any resulting article is probably going to result in a violation of the rules. By you.

If you link to an article, it is basically the same as if you made all of the statements in the article yourself. If the article mentions the terms of the offering, then you can't link to it from a non-terms communication (such as your website); and if it includes soft non-terms information, then you can't link to it from a tombstone communication. And if it includes misleading statements, you are now making those statements.

In general, if you (or your publicists) didn't participate in or suggest to a journalist that he or she write an article, it's not your problem. You aren't required to monitor the media or correct mistakes.

Regulation A—Up to $50 Million

Regulation A has existed for decades, but the JOBS Act made some changes to it that make it a very attractive option if you want to raise a larger amount—up to $50 million.

Title IV of the JOBS Act created something affectionately referred to as Regulation A+ that allows you to do a public offering for up to $50 million in all fifty states without having to do state level registrations.

To be able to use Regulation A+, you have to complete a fairly extensive filing with the SEC, and you have to have audited financials. The process takes about four months to complete and can cost $100,000 or more in legal and accounting fees. There are ongoing reporting requirements once the offering has been completed. Unaccredited investors may not invest more than 10 percent of the greater of their annual income or net worth.

This new and improved Regulation A has only been in effect since June 2015, but already quite a few companies have taken advantage of it.

NONPROFITS

As noted before, nonprofit organizations can issue securities. Section 3(a)(4) of the 1933 Securities Act exempts from the securities offering registration requirements "any security issued by a person organized and operated exclusively for religious, educational, benevolent, fraternal, charitable, or reformatory purposes and not for pecuniary profit, and no part of the net earnings of which inures to the benefit of any person, private stockholder, or individual."

In other words, securities issued by nonprofit organizations are exempt from the federal registration requirements. For example, RSF Social Finance is a nonprofit organization based in California. It raises capital in the form of loans that it invests in social enterprises. Because it's a nonprofit, it does not have to do any federal filings to be able to publicly offer an investment opportunity. However, it does still have to comply with state requirements.

Some states have exemptions similar to the federal exemption for nonprofits, which means that nonprofits can publicly offer investment opportunities without having to do any filings and without any limitations on who can invest and how much they can raise. Other states have exemptions but still require notice filings and fees, and they may place limits on how much can be raised and impose other requirements. Still other states have no exemption for nonprofit securities. Because RSF Social Finance wanted to be able to offer its investment opportunity in all fifty states, it researched the requirements for every state and completed the compliance requirements for every state. There were a few states where it took a lot of effort to convince the regulators to allow the offering in their state.

AGRICULTURAL CO-OPS

The agricultural cooperative exemption from the federal registration requirement is a bit obscure, but it's good to know about it in case it applies to you or someone you know.

Cooperatives that qualify for the farmer cooperative tax exemption of the Internal Revenue Code (Section 521) can issue securities without federal registration. This exemption also preempts the states from requiring state-level filings, so it makes a national securities offering relatively easy for these kinds of cooperatives. One of the best-known companies to use this exemption is Organic Valley, which has raised millions of dollars from investors throughout the United States using public offerings.

What Is a "Farmer Cooperative" Eligible for Tax Exemption under Section 521?

Tax-exempt farmer cooperatives are organizations (farmers, fruit growers, or similar associations organized and operated on a cooperative basis) that exist either for the purpose of marketing products or for the purpose of purchasing supplies. For marketing products, the organization has to return the proceeds of sales to the members (or other producers), less marketing expenses, on a basis related to the value (quantity) of the product they furnished. For purchasing supplies, the organization has to provide the supplies to members (or other persons) at actual cost, plus necessary expenses.

Organizations that meet these requirements can be classified as tax-exempt farmer cooperatives even if they have capital stock, provided that the stock meets certain requirements. The stock must be owned by the producers who market their products or purchase their supplies through the organization, unless it is nonvoting preferred stock. Holders of nonvoting preferred stock are not allowed to participate in the profits of the organization beyond fixed dividends. The dividend rate of the capital stock is not allowed to exceed the greater of the legal rate of interest in the state of incorporation or 8 percent annually.

Organizations that market the products of nonmembers can be tax-exempt farmer cooperatives if the amount of nonmember products does not exceed the value of member products. Similarly, the organization can purchase supplies and equipment for nonmembers as long as the value of the purchases does not exceed the value purchased for members and that value does not exceed 15 percent of the total value of purchases.

REGULATION S—OFFERS AND SALES THAT OCCUR OUTSIDE THE UNITED STATES

Regulation S is a safe-harbor exemption from federal registration requirements for certain offers and sales that occur outside the United States. Regulation S applies only if your investors are non-US persons physically located outside of the United States and only if you refrain from engaging in certain activities ("directed selling efforts") that might condition the US market for your securities, including certain forms of public advertising. In addition, you will need to make sure that you're complying with any applicable securities laws of the state in which your business is located and any countries where your potential investors reside.

WHO CAN MAKE THE OFFERING?

Let's say you go through the process necessary to allow you to legally solicit investors. Who can actually go out and sell those securities on your behalf? "Any person engaged in the business of effecting transactions in securities for the account of others" must register as a broker. So if someone offers to help you find investors and is paid a success fee or a commission, chances are that person will need to be a licensed broker. It is not always clear who will be considered a broker under state and federal law.

The factors that are considered by the regulators and the courts when determining whether someone meets the definition of a broker include whether the person provides investment advice, whether the person participates in negotiations, and whether the person is compensated based on a percentage of the transaction amount.

Federal law and most state laws have an exception to the requirement that anyone who represents an issuer in soliciting investors must be a licensed broker: if you are a director or officer or hold a similar position, in most cases you can solicit investors without having to be a licensed broker. Be sure to check applicable state law to determine who can legally make an offering and whether any filings are required.

INTEGRATION

The concept of integration is important to be familiar with when conducting securities offerings. The purpose of the integration requirements is to prevent someone from getting around the requirements of an exemption by doing more than one offering.

For example, let's say you decide to do a private offering under Rule 504 and you raise $4.5 million, and you include both accredited and unaccredited investors. Two months later, you decide to do another securities offering under Rule 506(c), and you raise $1.5 million.

Chances are, you are out of compliance. Why? Because the SEC will *integrate* the two offerings into one (i.e., treat them as if they were one offering) and then test whether the integrated offering meets the requirements of an exemption. It doesn't meet the requirements of Rule 504 because you raised $6 million total, which exceeds the $5 million maximum of Rule 504. It also doesn't meet the requirements of Rule 506(c) because you included unaccredited investors, which is not allowed under Rule 506(c).

How can you prevent two separate securities offerings from being integrated? The SEC looks at the following factors when determining whether two offerings should be integrated:

+ Whether the two offerings are part of a single plan of financing

+ Whether the two offerings are for the same class of securities
+ How close together the two offerings are in time
+ Whether the same type of payment for the securities is being received in both offerings
+ Whether the two offerings are for the same general purpose

The rules aren't very clear, so it may be difficult to tell whether two offerings are likely to be integrated by the SEC. Luckily, there is a safe harbor rule you can use to make sure that two offerings will not be integrated: as long as the end of one offering is separated by at least six months from the beginning of another offering, they will not be integrated. Similar requirements exist under state law.

Because of integration, it is important to decide at the beginning of your capital raising efforts which compliance strategy you plan to use. If you use one strategy and then want to switch to another, you may need to have a six-month separation between the final offering or sale in the first round and the first offering or sale in the second.

There are some exceptions to the integration rules. First, offerings using the new federal crowdfunding exemption will not be integrated with other offerings. So, for example, you could do a public offering under Rule 506(c) *and* a public offering under the federal crowdfunding exemption at the same time. Second, the SEC recently changed the requirements for the intrastate exemption so that it will not be integrated with any offering done before you use the intrastate exemption. This means that you can start an intrastate offering right after any other kind of offering.

RESALE OF SECURITIES

Most of the exemptions discussed in this chapter apply to the transaction and not to the security itself. So, for example, a securities offering may be exempt from registration under Rule 506(b), but that does not mean that the purchaser of the security can just turn around and resell the security to someone else; the resale of the security is not automatically exempt from registration. Some exemptions, however, such as the nonprofit exemption, apply to the security itself, which means that the security can be resold without having to meet the requirements of another exemption.

When the resale of a security is subject to further compliance requirements, it is called a *restricted security*. As it is unlikely that there will be much of a market for your securities, your investors will probably not be thinking about resale, so whether your securities are restricted or not is not of utmost importance. More information on resale restrictions is available on the readers' resources website.

YOUR NEXT STEP

Now that you know the options available to you, it's time to decide on your compliance strategy. This decision tree provides a basic decision-making framework you can use.

Keep in mind that this decision tree is oversimplified and does not include all of the details about what each compliance strategy entails. But it is a good starting point to help you narrow down your options.

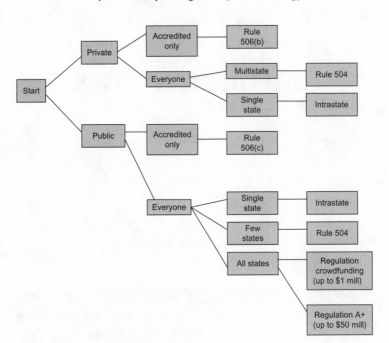

Once you choose a compliance strategy, be sure you understand the limitations on what you can do when you use that strategy and plan to file any necessary legal documents when they're due.

enroll investors

If you have worked your way through the first four steps in this book, by now you have most of your capital raising strategy in place. You know which investors you want to target, you know what you want to offer them, and you know your legal compliance strategy. Now you are ready to start talking to investors (assuming you have done any required filings and other legal compliance as discussed in step 4!).

You may think that if you chose a strategy that allows you to do public advertising, you don't have to worry so much about going out and talking to investors. You can just promote the heck out of your offering and people will invest, right? In my experience, it is usually not enough to publicly advertise your offering using mass communication tools. Even though you should certainly invest resources into a great advertising campaign, many investors will still need to hear from you personally before making the decision to invest. There are many reasons for this: (1) they may not see your advertising or may be too busy to notice it; (2) they may not think of themselves as an investor, so they may ignore the advertising, thinking it doesn't apply to them; (3) they may be interested in investing, but they keep procrastinating because they have other pressing things to attend to; or (4) they may be the kind of person who needs a personal connection before making an investment. These are just a few of the reasons why personal, one-on-one connections are so important, even if you are doing a public offering. And of course, if you are doing a private offering, they are the only option!

This step will give you some tools that will enable you to

1. Prepare to meet with investors
2. Ask for investor meetings
3. Know what to say in the meetings
4. Follow up after the meetings

WHAT TO PREPARE BEFORE YOU START MEETING WITH INVESTORS

Before you start meeting with investors, you may want to prepare one or more documents that you can share with them. What kinds of documents you prepare will depend on (1) whether any particular document is required by your legal compliance strategy, (2) what kinds of investors you're approaching (experienced, newbie, or something in between), and (3) whether you have a relationship with the investor or you're reaching out "cold."

Legal Requirements

If you are doing a public offering with one or more state registrations, you will create a prospectus (also sometimes called an *offering document*) that will be reviewed by the state regulators. This is the document you should share with potential investors. Most states allow you to create advertising materials in addition to the prospectus that you can also share with investors. (Sometimes the advertising must be approved in advance by the state regulators before you can use it.)

If you are doing a public offering under Title III of the JOBS Act, you will likely prepare some kind of disclosure document that will be posted on or downloadable from your fundraising page. You can also provide additional information on your page, such as a video, company brochures, photos, and testimonials. You can share all of these materials in one-on-one conversations with investors.

If you are raising money under Regulation A+, you will have an offering circular that is reviewed by the SEC that you will share with potential investors.

In private offerings, you are generally not required to prepare any particular type of disclosure document. However, to reduce the likelihood of lawsuits from disgruntled investors, you should provide to each investor all the information that a reasonable person would want to know before making an investment decision.

It is best to provide the same information to all potential investors. You would not want an investor to say that he never saw something that was shown to other investors. He could argue that he would have made a different investment decision if he had seen the information you shared with others.

When professional investors evaluate an investment opportunity, they conduct a process called *due diligence.* In this process, they ask for all kinds of information and background materials about the company and the offering. They usually don't require any kind of formal disclosure document; they just ask you to provide all of the information they request using an online private file-sharing service.

Nonprofessional investors may not ask you for any information at all. In that case, it's your responsibility to make sure you disclose material information to them.

How should you provide your disclosure information to potential investors? This decision is up to you. The safest thing to do is to provide a written document that includes information about the company, what you plan to use the money for, and the potential risks of investing, and have a way for investors to verify that they have received and reviewed the document.

What risks should you disclose? Anything that keeps you up at night about your business is something your potential investors would probably want to know about. If there is something that could be a direct threat to the business, such as a pending lawsuit, you should definitely disclose it. To see some sample risk disclosures, please visit the readers' resources website.

When investors actually agree to make an investment, they will often sign something called a *subscription agreement* or *investment agreement.* This document usually requires investors to acknowledge that they have had the opportunity to review relevant information about the company, that they have sufficient financial advice and/or experience to enter into the investment, and that they can afford a total loss of the investment. The subscription agreement provides you with some protection against lawsuits from disgruntled investors. However, if investors find out that there was relevant information about the company that was not disclosed before they made their investment decision, the company could be in violation of securities law and required, at a minimum, to return the funds raised.

If you've chosen a legal strategy that requires you to make an offering only to accredited investors (e.g., as required under Rule 506(b)), you should also prepare an investor questionnaire that you can give to potential investors before you make an offering to them, to ensure that they are accredited. (See a sample investor questionnaire on the readers' resources website.) Even if you are making an offering to both accredited and unaccredited investors, you may still need to know which of your investors are accredited and which are not, because that information must be reported on Form D and is required to ensure compliance with some state securities exemptions.

Other Documents

In addition to the documents that you're required to prepare under the applicable laws and regulations, you may want to prepare some other documents to show to potential investors. This section describes some of the most common documents that companies prepare when raising capital (examples of all of these can be found on the readers' resources website).

Executive Summary

One of the most common types of documents that companies prepare when offering an investment opportunity is called an *executive summary*. This is a very brief (one- to two-page) document that gives the basic information about the company and the offering. Ideally it is put together by someone with graphic design skills so that it looks nice.

Preparing an executive summary is a great exercise for honing your message about your business. You need to be able to say in as few words as possible what your business does and why someone should care. Even if you never share it with a potential investor, take the time to prepare an executive summary and show it to someone who doesn't know much about your business. After she reads it, ask her to explain to you what your business does. If she is unable to articulate it and seems unsure, you need to clarify your message. Keep bouncing it off people until everyone who reads it understands immediately what your business does. This is a great exercise for marketing as well as for raising capital!

An executive summary usually contains the following information:

+ Company name and contact information
+ Brief summary of what the business does
+ The need the business serves
+ Who the customers are and the size of the market
+ Revenue model—how the company makes money
+ The unique value proposition of the company compared to its competitors

153

+ The team
+ How much the company is raising
+ What is being offered (details of the security)
+ Call to action—that is, whom to contact if interested in investing

An executive summary is a great tool to share with potential investors whom you don't know well or whom you are approaching cold, because they can skim it quickly to determine if they are interested.

Pitch Deck

A *pitch deck* is a set of slides (usually created in Power-Point or a similar program) describing your company and your investment offering. If you like to use slides to help you make a presentation, this is a great tool to have handy while you are meeting with an investor. You can show the slides on your tablet or laptop while you're talking about your offering. You can use the slides to provide visuals to supplement your verbal description—for example, to show what your product looks like or what your team looks like.

If you plan to share the pitch deck while you're giving a presentation, it is crucial to minimize text in the slides. No one can read a slide while simultaneously listening to a presentation. It's okay to include some text, but be sure to read it aloud or give the viewer time to read it while you stop talking. The more you rely on high-impact images and the less you rely on text, the better the presentation will be understood. Again, it is worth having a professional graphic designer make the slides look great.

In the world of Silicon Valley–style investing, a pitch deck is a must; VCs and professional angels expect you to use one to make a formal pitch. There are endless discussions online about how to make the best possible pitch deck. If you are not pitching to Silicon Valley–style investors, you do not need to prepare a pitch deck. Create one only if you think it will help you when you talk to investors. Some investors may be much more comfortable with an informal conversation than a formal presentation.

If you do prepare a pitch deck, you can create two versions: one with very little text that you use in conjunction with a verbal presentation, and one with more text that you can e-mail to potential investors to help them determine whether they are interested in discussing the opportunity further. In either case, the deck should consist of ten to fifteen slides and contain information similar to an executive summary. An executive summary may be preferable because it usually takes less time to review.

Remember that people have a lot of things competing for their attention, so anything you send them should be simple, easy to scan quickly, and professional looking. It's a cliché but true that you have only one chance to make a first impression, and a poorly designed pitch deck or executive summary can send the message that you don't care enough about how you present yourself and your business. It's worthwhile to invest in making a great first impression so that you can get your foot in the door and get that face-to-face meeting.

Term Sheet

A *term sheet* is a detailed description of what you are offering to the investor (e.g., preferred stock, convertible notes—whatever you designed in step 3). You probably wouldn't show this to an investor until he or she has expressed serious interest in investing. This is the document you use to get down to brass tacks: What exactly is the investor getting for his or her money?

If you're talking to professional investors, they will likely want a say in the terms of the investment, so any term sheet you show to them would be considered a proposal subject to negotiation. For nonprofessional investors who are less likely to negotiate terms, it can be very helpful for them to see the details of exactly what you are offering. They may want to show it to their financial advisor or other trusted person before making a decision.

Private Placement Memorandum

Some companies prepare a document called a *private placement memorandum* (PPM) when raising capital in a private offering. These are not legally required, but they are prepared when the company raising funds wants to thoroughly protect itself from potential liability from investors claiming they did not receive all material information before making an investment decision. PPMs are usually prepared by law firms and can cost tens of thousands of dollars. If you have made sure that you've provided all material information to your potential investors (and document that you did), a PPM can be overkill.

PPMs usually include

+ Investor qualifications and requirements
+ Risk factors
+ Company financial information
+ Company history and current operations
+ A description of any intellectual property owned by the company
+ Team
+ Existing sources of financing
+ Description of the offering
+ Any other information that would be material to an investor's decision about whether to invest

Other Options

You can prepare whatever you want to show to potential investors (as long as it isn't misleading or false). Why not get creative? How about a poem, a collage, or a drawing? Think about what would be most compelling for your ideal investors and pour your heart into creating it. The right investors will be thrilled that you are not boring them with a slide deck!

HOW TO ASK FOR THE MEETING

Okay, so you have the materials in place that you are going to share with potential investors, or you've decided that you don't need to prepare any materials and plan to rely solely on your gift of gab.

Now is the time to start getting some appointments in the calendar! The more conversations you have, the faster you will find your ideal investors and hone your message so that it really speaks to them. Think of your investors as a particular breed of dog and your investment offering as a dog whistle that is irresistible to them but unappealing to all other dogs.

But first, you have to get their attention. Your potential investors are likely to be busy people—how do you get them to say yes to a lunch date or videoconference appointment?

Your ideal investors are people who are passionate about the same things you are. When you ask them for a meeting, you should emphasize that the reason you are asking is that you know that what you are doing is well suited to what you believe they care about.

They may be very excited to have the opportunity to talk to you about your business because you are an expert on something that is important to them. For example, let's say you have built a business around your passion for providing nutritious, healthy food that busy parents can easily feed their kids. There are people out there who are really interested in learning how you do this, what lessons you're learning, how you source your ingredients, the most up-to-date science on kids' nutrition, the state of the food industry in our country, the name of the best pediatrician in the area who specializes in kids with food allergies, and so on. They would be thrilled to talk with you about all of these topics.

Or maybe they would just love the opportunity to talk with someone who shares their passions and values.

When asking for a meeting, you want to let potential investors know what the meeting will be about while at the same time making it clear that they should not feel any pressure or obligation; this is just a chance to talk and learn more about what you're working on.

Here is script I adapted from a training by Nina Simons, president and cofounder of Bioneers and former president of Seeds of Change, that you can use to make it clear that you want to talk about an investment while still making people feel very comfortable and giving them an "out" if it's not a good fit.

> I'm not sure if you know about the business I've been working on, but I'm really excited about it, and knowing what I know about you, I think it might be something that could be of interest to you.
>
> I'm looking for some people to come in and support the growth of the business, and I'm wondering if you'd like to go out to lunch so I can tell you more about it.
>
> I realize it may or may not be a good fit for you. And if it's not, no harm no foul. But I would love to share it with you and see what you think.

WHAT TO SAY IN THE MEETING

Start with Questions

Start the meeting by asking your potential investor some questions about what's important to her. Instead of jumping right in and presenting the investment opportunity, ask how she feels about what kinds of opportunities are out there, the things that she's been investing in that she feels really good about, and the things that she doesn't feel so good about.

By asking these questions, you will demonstrate that you genuinely care about where she is coming from and what's important to her. This will put her at ease and help her feel that you are not just looking at her as a source of funding but as a potential partner and supporter, and as a complete human being. Also, getting answers to these questions will help you determine whether what you're offering is truly a good fit for what this person is looking for.

Once you've spent some time listening to her, decide whether it makes sense to move forward with making your offer. If you get the sense that there is a potential fit, move forward. If not, don't bother making an offer, although you should ask for referrals to people she knows who might be interested.

Share Your Vision

Noha Waibsnaider, the founder of Peeled Snacks, says, "Investors want to pretend to invest in people. They're motivated to make an investment when they see your passion for the business you're building. Sure the numbers and the financials are important, but what really gets them over the finish line is your vision and your commitment to the mission of your company. Sell the big vision, not the details."[32]

If after asking some questions and really listening to the answers, you decide to move forward with making an offer, start by talking about your vision and mission. Entrepreneurs are often tempted to jump quickly into the nuts and bolts of the business model, the revenue projections, the details of the product or service, and so on. What I've heard over and over again from both entrepreneurs and investors is that if an investor has really bought into your vision, the details aren't so important. Yes, investors will want information on all of those things, but for them to even take the time to listen to the details, they need to be sold on the vision, mission, and big picture of the business.

Before meeting with investors, practice making a short presentation of your vision of what the business is all about, what its purpose is, what impact you see it making in the world, how you see it growing over time, and why you're so passionate about it. Practice your presentation with friends and supporters so that it becomes second nature. Your presentation shouldn't be a canned speech but something that comes from your heart.

Also, because you've spent some time listening to the potential investor at the beginning of the meeting, you can tailor what you say to emphasize the things that you know are important to her. Of course you want to make sure this is genuine—you may customize what you focus on, but you should never misrepresent anything to fit what you think the investor wants to hear.

Be Authentic

A lot of entrepreneurs think that to impress an investor, they need to pretend to be someone they're not. That is not a good idea and can backfire. First of all, people can usually sense when someone's not being authentic. They may not be totally conscious of what is going on, but something will not feel right, and they will not invest.

Second, you have a much better chance of attracting investors who are going to be a great fit for you if you're honest about who you are and what's important to you. Just as lying on your online dating profile only leads to heartache when you end up attracting someone based on deception, the same holds true in the world of capital raising.

Don't water down your message—show your passion! Be proud of what makes you unique and, yes, maybe a little quirky. Very few people want to invest in something generic. Highlight what makes you, your company, and your product or service truly special and inspired.

Your presentation should make it clear that you are passionate about your business. Passion is attractive because it demonstrates commitment; this is not something that you are going to give up on at the first sign of hardship!

Maybe there's something about your personal story of what led you to develop this business that makes you all the more passionate and committed. For example, I have a client whose children have multiple allergies. She became passionate about finding healthy foods for them and built her whole business around that. The story behind her business is really interesting, and it adds to her credibility in the eyes of potential investors.

Share What Makes You Special

By sharing your vision and your passion, you have already created a great impression. Now is the time to do a little shameless self-promotion. Share information and stories about yourself that demonstrate your intelligence, experience, and ability to get things done.

It is also essential to make sure that your potential investors know that you have integrity, that you're going to be a careful steward of their money, and that you will always act with the highest ethics. These attributes are important to investors and not necessarily common in the world of business. If these attributes come naturally to you, you may take them for granted, but you need to remember that they add value to your investment proposition and so should be emphasized in your presentation. Share stories or examples of how important integrity is to you.

Talk about Your Community

Is your business tied to a community or tribe—maybe craft beer drinkers, environmentalists, fair trade supporters, holistic healers? If so, this is a huge plus, so be sure to talk about it. First of all, if you have a community or tribe that is passionate about your business, the business is more likely to be successful, making it a less risky investment. Also, a lot of investors love the idea of being part of a tribe. You can design creative ways for your investors to go beyond just being a source of funding to being an important part of your tribe. Maybe they get to sit on a special advisory committee that tastes all your products before they are marketed publicly; maybe they get priority seating at your restaurant or an invitation to a special VIP event". Many investors may value the opportunity to become part of a community of passionate, like-minded people more highly than the financial return on their investment.

Make Your Offer

Once you have shared your vision, your passion, what makes you uniquely qualified to run this business, your integrity, your commitment, and your community, you can tell the potential investor what you are offering.

What if the investor is interested but doesn't like certain terms of the offering you designed? It is fine to negotiate as long as you stay true to the underlying principles of your offering. Is it okay to have each investor negotiate different terms? In a private offering, this is generally fine, but you should be sure to disclose to all investors the fact that each investor may have different terms. In a public offering, you will usually need to stick to the same terms for everyone because you decide on the terms up front before you start publicly advertising, and any changes would require amendments to the offering documents.

Get a Yes or a No

If you possibly can, try to end the meeting with a clear answer and not an "I'll think about it." It is no fun to have to repeatedly nag someone to make a decision. Of course, if she expresses interest but has a legitimate reason why she needs a little more time to decide (e.g., she wants to talk to an advisor or spouse), that's fine. But if you get the sense that she is trying to avoid saying no because she doesn't want to hurt your feelings, you can say something like this:

> I so appreciate your taking the time to listen to me tell you about this investment opportunity. I'm in the process of talking to a lot of potential investors and would like to close this funding round as soon as possible. If you're interested in pursuing this, let's agree on the next step to closing your investment (for example, do you need to talk to someone or see my financials for the last five years?). If you're not interested, please do go ahead and let me know so I don't waste your time following up. Believe me, if the answer is no, it is much better for me to know that now! And of course, no hard feelings if this isn't right for you right now.

Be Prepared to Walk Away

As you go through the capital raising process, commit to yourself that you will walk away from a potential investor if the fit does not feel right. This can happen for many reasons. For example, you get a sense from the investor that he or she has a vision for the future of your business that is not consistent with yours. Or he or she is already pressuring you to lower your wages and stop paying 1 percent of your revenues to charity when those things are really important to you. Or maybe it's just a gut feeling that this person is not a good fit.

Janie Hoffman, the founder of Mamma Chia, says,

> We were always very clear about who we are. For example, we joined 1% for the Planet, which requires a commitment that we donate 1 percent of our gross revenues to environmental nonprofits. This sent a clear message to potential investors about our values and made it easier for us to attract investors who shared our values. We were very selective about who we were willing to take money from. We probably said no to ten times more investors than we said yes to. It wasn't worth it to us to bring on investors who were not supportive of our vision.[33]

Being prepared to walk away reduces the chances that you will end up with a horror story situation in which you lose control, you get fired from your own business, your investor makes your life miserable, and the like. I have heard lots of these stories, and believe me, you don't want them to happen to you!

Another benefit of being prepared to walk away and really owning that mind-set is that potential investors will be far more attracted to your offer because they will sense that they have to work to be accepted into your inner circle. You are evaluating them just as much as they are evaluating you.

Special Considerations for Newbie Investors

As you know, I strongly recommend approaching all kinds of investors, including those who may have never invested in a small business before and don't think of themselves as investors. These people can be amazing supporters and allies. The challenge is that these folks have been told for so long that investing is something done by VCs and hedge fund managers, not regular people like them, that they sometimes need some education to help them even consider an investment in a small business. Here are some questions they might ask and how you can respond.

Is this crowdfunding?

It depends on what you mean by crowdfunding. In one very common type of crowdfunding, a business posts some kind of a project on a crowdfunding site like Kickstarter and solicits donations. Donors are often promised something in return for their donation, like a T-shirt or a thank-you note.

That is not what I'm doing. I'm actually raising investment capital. This means that if you decide to invest and things go as planned, you will receive a financial return on your investment—just like you do when you put your money in the bank or invest in the stock market.

How is that legal? I thought it was illegal for small businesses to ask for investment from regular people.

Some lawyers and financial advisors might tell you that, but it's actually not the case. My offering is being done in compliance with both state and federal securities law.

I'm not an investor.

Actually, if you're like a majority of the US population, you *are* an investor! You may not think of yourself as one, but if you have retirement accounts, bank accounts, or mutual funds, you are an investor! And you have options about where you can put your investment dollars.

Are you paying a market-rate return?

The term *market rate* is very subjective and hard to define. What I'm offering is an [X] percent annual payment in the form of [interest or profit distribution]. This return is much better than what you would get if you put your money into a certificate of deposit at a bank, where you can currently get [Y] percent interest. Of course, there is more risk if you invest in my business because your investment is not insured by the FDIC like a bank deposit is. The return I am paying to my investors is based on my projections about the future of my business. I want to pay enough to fairly compensate my investors while also making sure that I don't promise more than I can realistically afford to pay and still keep my business healthy.

Remember that all investment is risky! Even an investment in an indexed stock mutual fund can be quite volatile and is affected by factors that are completely out of the investors' control.

Also, there is a lot of hype about what a market-rate return is. For example, you may hear some investment advisors say you can expect a 6–8 percent return if you keep your money in the stock market over the long term. The reality is that the Dow Jones Industrial Average annual return for the last ten years is less than 3.25 percent, and past returns cannot be used to predict the future. Some experts are saying that the world's financial markets are likely overvalued by at least $20 trillion due to the inclusion of fossil fuel assets that can't be used without destroying the planet, and a recent analysis cited in the *Wall Street Journal* predicts a 17 percent stock market drop caused by a pulling back from liberalized global trade.

How will I get my money back?

You may have heard of the venture capital model of investment where the investor gets paid back when the company is sold or goes public. There are some stories of investors making millions when they got lucky and invested early in a company that ended up going big. In reality, the majority of investments that depend on a big sale or IPO don't succeed, and the investors end up losing money.

[Choose from one of the two options here depending on which one is true for you:]

That model doesn't fit my business. I expect to grow modestly every year, and I have no immediate plans to sell to a larger business or do an IPO. That's why I am compensating my investors by sharing my profits. My plan is that by the [Xth] year, I will be able to pay back my investors their original investment, in addition to the annual share of profits.

[Or]

I do expect to sell my business someday, but I will not sell at any cost. I will only sell to a buyer who I believe will stay true to the mission of the business, and I want the freedom to choose whether or not to sell based on what I believe to be in the best interests of the business and its long-term impact. However, in the meantime, I plan to compensate my investors by sharing my profits.

So are you saying this is a "lifestyle business"?

I have heard some people categorize businesses that do not follow the venture capital model as "lifestyle businesses." This seems to mean a business that grows modestly and is not shooting for a fast exit at a high valuation. In that sense, I guess you could say that my business is a lifestyle business. I have noticed that some people think that these kinds of business are not "investable." Nothing could be further from the truth! Investing in a business that shares a reasonable return from its profits every year can be a great investment, compared to an investment that gambles on that one-in-a-million chance of a super-profitable exit!

Isn't this a risky investment?

Of course, all investment is risky to some extent, and not all small businesses succeed. You should invest only what you can afford to lose.

But here are some things to keep in mind when evaluating risk:

+   Look at your whole portfolio and remember that diversification mitigates risk. If almost all of your investments are in the stock market, investing in a small business whose success is not tied directly to the ups and downs of the public markets can be a good way to diversify your portfolio. Think about it—almost all of most Americans' investments are in giant multinational public companies. But 99 percent of US businesses are small private companies that account for half of all employment and half of all production. Why put all of your investment dollars into only half of the economy?

+ The stock market has been likened to a casino; it has become very opaque, trading is increasingly conducted by algorithms, and financial instruments have become so far removed from the real economy that it is hard to trust that it will continue to be a safe place to put your nest egg.

+ Maybe you've heard Warren Buffett's advice: "Never invest in a business you cannot understand." Most investors not only don't understand the businesses they're investing in; they don't even know *what* businesses they're investing in! They just let their fund managers make all the decisions and hope for the best. Why not invest in a business that you know and understand?

+ Most of our investments are made through intermediaries (often more than one) like stock brokers, fund managers, and investment advisors. When you invest directly in a business, you eliminate the fees and percentages taken by these intermediaries, and there is more transparency about what you are actually investing in.

+ A business is all about the people who run it. When you invest in a small business, you're investing in the founder based on your opinion of her commitment, integrity, and abilities. A small business owner is generally going to be much more committed to her business's success than a CEO of a multinational public company. CEOs move around from company to company and get their golden parachutes when they leave. Entrepreneurs usually start their businesses to express their most dearly held dreams and passions. Their business is their baby, so they will stick with it through thick and thin.

+ When you invest in a business based on your relationship with the owner, that owner is going to feel personally responsible for your investment dollars. The last thing she wants is for someone she knows to lose money by investing in her business. She will do almost anything to avoid having to tell her investors that she has lost their money or is unable to pay them as much as she had promised. When you invest in a faceless multinational corporation, there is no similar feeling of personal responsibility to the investors.

Besides the financial returns, what are the other benefits of investing in your business?

When you invest in a small business, you often get benefits that go beyond purely financial returns.

These vary depending on the particular investment and business, but they often include

+ Having the pride of knowing that you helped a business that's important to your community

171

+ Being able to tell your friends and colleagues that you invested in a business they may know and love
+ Being part of a community of investors with similar values
+ Having the opportunity to learn from the business owner about the details of the business
+ Providing support to the business owner when she needs it—advice, contacts, business referrals, and so on
+ Having some ability to affect the success of the business as a customer and as a source of support
+ Being invited to special events
+ Being recognized publicly as a supporter of small business
+ Receiving discounts and perks
+ Knowing that your investment dollars are benefitting something that is having a positive impact in the world

Remember, all investments have an impact; what impact do you want your investments to have? When you invest in a mutual fund of public company stocks, does that create any positive impact in your community or on things that are important to you?

Investing in small businesses allows you to invest in the real economy in a business that employs people and provides useful goods and services. When you invest in public company stocks, your money doesn't even go to that company—it just goes to the previous owner of the stock!

Why not use some of your investment dollars to invest in things that are important to you—community gathering places, alternative energy, businesses that create good local jobs? Imagine if everyone moved just a small percentage of their investment dollars to small businesses creating a positive impact in the world—we could create a better world by simply being more mindful about where we put our money.

FOLLOWING UP AFTER THE MEETING

As discussed earlier, it is best to get an answer at the meeting. It is inevitable, however, that some potential investors will be interested but will not be ready to make a decision. Be sure those folks are on your e-mail list and send them regular updates about your business so that you stay top of mind. Set a calendar reminder to follow up with a phone call every few weeks. Persistence can really pay off. Of course, be very kind about it, and remember that you are offering them a great opportunity! You are not begging them for a handout. In the final step, we will cover this topic in a lot more detail.

A NOTE ABOUT FINDERS

You may be thinking, *But I don't want to have to talk to potential investors! Can't I just pay someone to do it for me?*

There are people out there (often called "finders") who will tell you that they will find investors for you for a fee. Usually they will charge an up-front fee plus a commission. Generally speaking, it is illegal for someone to do this without being a licensed broker and a member of FINRA (the regulatory body for the financial industry). So if you are considering hiring someone to help you, make sure that he or she is a member in good standing with FINRA (http://brokercheck.finra.org/).

Although it is certainly nice to have someone help you find investors, you need to be realistic about whether this is a good strategy. Unfortunately, I have heard many stories of finders charging large up-front fees and then failing to deliver a single investor. If you are considering using a finder, make sure you have evidence (e.g., satisfied former clients, past successes) that this person can actually help.

And don't hire a finder as a way to avoid having to talk to investors. Potential investors will want to get to know you, and you will want to get to know them as well, to make sure they are a good fit. Use the exercises in step 6 to tackle your fears about talking to investors—you can do it!

address obstacles head on

If you've worked through the first five steps, you should be more than ready to go out and start talking to investors.

Having worked with clients raising capital for over ten years, I have noticed a phenomenon that happens sometimes when everything they need is in place. All of a sudden, obstacles of all kinds start popping up, and somehow days go by without a single investor conversation.

I have seen entrepreneurs take far longer than may have been necessary to reach their fundraising goals because they kept finding excuses to avoid actually going out and asking for investment. Fears and doubts often are what underlie these excuses.

I believe that you can address most of the obstacles that come up during the capital raising process by working on your mind-set, and that's what you'll be doing in this step. Although it is natural to feel some nervousness and discomfort about talking to potential investors, there are some things you can do that will help you feel the fear but then do it anyway.

It is just as important to consciously cultivate your state of mind for raising capital as it is to create a great pitch presentation. Too many entrepreneurs approach investors as if they are begging for a handout, rather than offering something of huge value. This does not tend to inspire confidence. The more you can do to believe fully in the value of what you are offering to investors, the more successful you will be.

YOUR WHY

Go back and review the work you did in step 1. Remember why you started this business in the first place. Remember the unique value and impact your business creates. The world needs you to contribute your unique genius and gifts— raising money to bring your dream to fruition is your moral obligation! Keep reminding yourself that this is not just about you; it is about all the people who will benefit when you are able to grow your business on your own terms.

YOUR MIND-SET

This step contains exercises that will help you recognize the value of what you are offering to investors and understand their frustrations, enabling you to see that you may be the answer to their prayers.

Many entrepreneurs think that if they can't promise a 30x return (VC-speak for returning thirty times the investor's original investment), no investor will give them the time of day.

This is absolutely not true. As we've discussed throughout this book, the 30x return is little more than a myth. The average investor is lucky to make a 3–5 percent annual return on his or her investments (and much less if the money is parked at a bank). You must compare yourself to the reality of "market-rate returns" and not the hype.

Plus, investors care about a lot more than financial returns. Among other things, they care about

+ Being able to trust the leaders of the companies they invest in
+ Reasonable level of risk
+ Transparency
+ Being part of a special community or tribe
+ Being able to tell their friends and acquaintances about the cool thing they invested in
+ Values alignment
+ Cool perks
+ Low to no intermediary fees

Studies have demonstrated that investors care about how their investments make them feel.[34] A majority of investors say that it is important to them that their investments are in alignment with their values.[35]

And a quick word about risk. What makes an investment risky? No one can predict the future, so risk is mostly about perception. First, *all* investments have some degree of risk associated with them, and investors generally understand that (and they are required to sign documents acknowledging their understanding of that fact). What investors consider more or less risky is influenced by numerous factors, such as whether they know and trust the company leadership, whether they understand the business model, whether they believe the business model is consistent with global trends (e.g., renewable energy versus fossil fuels), and the like. There is really no fool-proof way to evaluate risk. You just need to connect with investors who perceive an investment in your company as offering the right combination of risk and return (both financial and nonfinancial) for their particular personality and preferences.

Good investments are not easy to find. People are searching for investment opportunities in companies whose leaders have integrity, who will be good stewards of their mone, and who are dedicated to their company's success. You can offer that to your investors.

Imagine that you sell cakes. You're getting ready to sell your cakes at the farmers market for the first time, and you start worrying that your cakes are not perfect. You notice all the things about them that could be better. Then you go to the farmers market. You look at all the other cakes that are being sold, and you try samples of them. They are stale, too dry, and really not very good at all! All of a sudden you realize—people are going to be thrilled with your cakes even though they aren't perfect!

It's the same thing with offering an investment opportunity. You can dwell on all the "bad" things about what you're offering: a return nowhere near as high as what most VCs are looking for, no guarantee that the investors will actually make money, no one on the team with a Stanford MBA . . . But if you look around at what investors have to choose from, you may quickly realize that what you are offering will be quite attractive to the right investor.

Here is an example that proves my point: Imagine an equity investment in which investors might or might not receive any return on the investment (it is completely up to the discretion of the company's board of directors); the investors have no voting rights; the investors can never sell their equity at a profit or receive a windfall in the case of an IPO or sale of the company; and if the investors ever want to get their original investment back, they can request it, but the redemption is not guaranteed, and the investor must wait five years before even having a chance of getting the original investment back. This sounds like a challenging investment to raise money for, right? Well, the company that offers this investment (Equal Exchange) raises millions of dollars every time it opens up this opportunity, and has more people who want to invest than it can accept.

Here's another example: Imagine a start-up retail store that has no customers or even a location yet, which offers an equity investment with no voting rights and a high likelihood that investors will not see a dime for seven years, and even then the annual dividend is only 3 percent. This investment opportunity was offered by People's Community Market and resulted in a raise of approximately $3.4 million.

Why are people so interested in these investment opportunities, which VCs would consider laughable and completely unworthy of their consideration? Because these companies offer the right combination of values alignment, trustworthiness, and financial return for their ideal investors.

Chances are that what you uniquely have to offer will be a great fit for some subset of the population (i.e., your ideal investors).

Remember that your unique combination of skills, experience, relationships, values, and resources is not something that an investor can easily find. What you are offering will be a huge gift for the right investor and will have value far beyond the amount of money you are asking for.

Many people are in pain about the lack of investment opportunities that meet their criteria. There are investors out there just waiting to hear from you!

Here is something I want you to write down and keep in your journal or on a sticky note on your computer:

My investors need ME just as much as I need THEM.

EXERCISES

Kick Limiting Beliefs to the Curb

We *always* have beliefs swirling around in our head, but we may not always be consciously aware of them. Your unconscious beliefs may be undermining your capital raising success. Imagine approaching an investor with these beliefs running through your head:

> She would be crazy to invest in my business, but I desperately need this money! I hope she takes pity on me!

Compare that to this alternative set of beliefs:

> I am so excited about the business that I'm growing. Not only do we have a solid business model, but it will

also make a really great impact on the world. While I know I can't guarantee that my investors will get paid back or make a good return (pretty much no investment can), I *can* guarantee that I will work my butt off to make this business a success. How many other investment opportunities out there come with the level of commitment, integrity, and stewardship that I can deliver?

To work on your limiting beliefs, sit in a comfortable place where you won't be distracted. Close your eyes. Have a pen and paper nearby.

Picture yourself at a networking event. You see someone whom you've met before, and you think that person could be a great investor for you. If possible, picture someone you actually know whom you would like to bring on as an investor. Imagine walking over to that person, starting a conversation, and talking to her about whether she would be interested in investing in your business.

Write down every thought that comes into your head when you picture talking to that person about investing in your business. Don't analyze or censor—just do a brain dump of everything that comes up.

Now picture yourself several months in the future. Today is the day that you reached your fundraising goal. You have all of the money that you set out to raise. Now what? What thoughts come up about the next steps for your business? About your relationship with your investors? About how this will affect your personal life? What excites you? What worries you?

Write down every thought that comes into your head when you picture having raised all the money you set out to raise. Again, don't think too much—just do a brain dump of everything that comes up.

This exercise may have helped you see that you have limiting beliefs that can hold you back from success with raising capital.

In your journal, draw a line down the center of a page. On the left side, write down all the limiting beliefs you identified. On the right side, next to each limiting belief, write down a more positive, empowering thought. The table here shows some examples.

Unconscious Thought	Rational Thought
Who am I to ask someone to invest in my business?	I know my business brings value to the world. If I don't grow my business, I won't be able to serve all the people who would benefit. The right investor will see the value in that and be excited to support me.
What if I lose their money?	Everyone who invests knows there is a possibility they will lose their money. The chances that this will happen are low because I will do what it takes to make the business successful. If things don't work out, my investors will know I did the best I could.
Once I have investors, I'll be so stressed all the time about whether they will get what I promised.	Having investors will give me an incentive to stay as focused as possible and do what it takes to make my business a success. Also, I'll have a built-in source of support when I need advice or resources.

Unconscious Thought	Rational Thought
Once I have the money, I'll have to hire salespeople, and I always do such a bad job choosing the right people. I'll end up having tons of issues with my employees.	I can use some of the money I raise to hire an expert to help me with the hiring process.
I can't go out and ask for investment until I fix my website.	If I wait to raise money until everything in my business is perfect, I'll be stuck playing small forever. What I have now is good enough.
I don't have time for this!	Without investment, I can't take my business where I want it to go. Every minute I spend on this is worth it. And raising capital is a great growth opportunity!

Recognize that limiting beliefs are simply thoughts and that you can choose not to listen to them. Thank them for their input and tell them they are no longer needed.

Once you drag your limiting beliefs out into the light of day, you can loosen their grip on you by noticing how ridiculous most of them are!

Remember that being confident does not mean that you never have any fears or doubts. It means that you are willing to take the next step even though you may feel shaky or nervous.

Raising money is not something one does every day, and it requires you to be vulnerable and face possible rejection. Of course this will not always be comfortable. Getting uncomfortable means that you are pushing your limits; try to welcome those feelings of discomfort as a sign that you are moving in the right direction to grow your business to the next level.

Make it a regular practice to expose and debunk those beliefs that don't serve you well.

Put Yourself in the Investor's Shoes

Do you have any investments like a retirement account, mutual fund, or a savings account? If so, this exercise shouldn't be too difficult because you are an investor! You may not be very different from your ideal investor.

1. Picture your ideal investor.
2. Imagine that you are your ideal investor. Try to put yourself in his or her shoes and imagine what it feels like to be this person.
3. Now imagine that you wake up in the morning and you're worried. You have some money to invest, but you're not sure what to do with it. You open up today's *Wall Street Journal* and see these headlines (these are actual recent headlines with slight edits):
   "Dow Ends Rough Week"
   "Chasing Hot Returns in the Latest New Funds Can Be a Dumb Idea"
   "Amid Increased Volatility, Investors Uneasy"
   "S&P 500 Fell 0.7%, Outperforming Hedge Funds, Which Lost 1%"
   "U.S. Equities Expected to Shed More Than 17% as Global Trade Slows"
4. Now imagine that you are tired of losing sleep over this: you are going to put some attention to this issue.

You start by writing down your most important criteria for choosing an investment. What do you write down? The following are some examples. Try to come up with your own as you imagine what your ideal investor is thinking.

+ I want some investments that are not tied to the crazy volatility of Wall Street.
+ I don't want to pay fees to professional wealth managers.
+ I want my investments to create good jobs in my community or at least in America.
+ I want to invest in people who have integrity and are not just trying to make a buck no matter who they hurt in the process.

5. Now step back into your own shoes. Write down how an investment in your business lines up with your ideal investor's criteria.

Take Care of Yourself

Commit to yourself that you will make self-care a regular habit while you're raising capital. Write in your journal what you will do to feel your best during the process. Here are some examples:

+ Massage
+ Relaxing walks
+ Cuddling with your pet
+ Meditation
+ A daily ritual that reminds you of how awesome you are
+ Whatever makes you feel a ton of self-love!

Block out time in your calendar to do these things on a regular basis. If during the capital raising process you treat yourself with as much love as you would your most cherished best friend, you will show up as confident and relaxed when you meet with potential investors, and you will naturally attract investors who resonate with the best of what you have to offer.

A FINAL WORD

Nina Simons of Bioneers says that "fundraising is like cultivating a garden." Take the time to get to know potential investors and those who may be able to introduce you to investors. It can take several touch points before an investor says yes. During this process, treat the investor as a whole person, not just as a wallet that you're trying to get into. Everyone, including investors, wants to be seen for the entire person he is and appreciated for all that he has to offer.

conclusion: pulling it all together— your go-to-market plan

If you've worked through the six steps of this book, you should have a complete capital raising plan in place:

1. You are clear on your goals and values, which include
   a. Your why
   b. Your vision for your business
   c. Your nonnegotiables
   d. Your business goals
   e. How much you want to raise
2. You've identified your ideal investors, including
   a. Their demographics and psychographics
   b. Your ideal relationship with them
   c. Where you will find them
   d. What they're looking for in an investment
3. You've designed your offer, including
   a. What instrument to offer (debt or equity)
   b. Your investors' economic rights
   c. Your investors' governance rights (if any)

    d. How your investors will exit

    e. What perks, if any, will go along with the investment

    f. The legal documents that reflect your offering

4. You've decided on a legal compliance strategy, including

    a. Whether you will publicly advertise the offering

    b. Whether you will include accredited investors only or open the offering to everybody

    c. What states you will make the offering in

5. You've prepared to enroll investors, including

    a. Creating the documents you'll share with potential investors

    b. Knowing how you'll ask for meetings

    c. Knowing what you'll say in the meetings

    d. Knowing how you'll follow up

6. You've created a plan to deal with mind-set obstacles.

Now is the time to implement your plan, which means reaching out to potential investors. Depending on your legal compliance strategy, this may include an advertising campaign, and it will certainly include one-on-one conversations.

The best way to begin is to block out time in your calendar to focus on raising capital. If you don't commit to spending specific hours in your day on this, you will probably find a million other things to do, such as balancing your checkbook or cleaning out your office supply cabinet!

Entrepreneurs who reach their capital raising goals quickly may spend as much as 80 percent of their work time devoted to reaching out to investors. This is a numbers game.

The more people you talk to, the more quickly you'll get it done. Commit to talking to a certain number of potential investors each week. If you have a meeting that doesn't go well, congratulate yourself for getting through it, call a supportive friend, and get right back into the next meeting.

I recommend finding one or more capital raising buddies who can keep you accountable and give you feedback. Be sure to surround yourself with positive can-do people and avoid naysayers.

Set yourself a deadline by which you want to achieve your goal. A shorter deadline will inspire you to throw yourself into it with everything you have, *and* it will motivate potential investors to make a quick decision. Get it done fast so you can get back to running your business and put that cash to work.

Know in advance that you will almost certainly meet with potential investors who will be critical, tell you to change your business model, or think you are nuts. Don't let that affect your confidence and your commitment to raise money on your own terms. Your offering will appeal only to your ideal investors. It will not appeal to everyone. That is part of the process. Don't waste your time with those who don't share your vision and passion.

THERE HAS NEVER BEEN A BETTER TIME TO DO THIS!

A new generation, the millennials, is coming of investment age, and they are looking for you! As the baby boomer generation passes away, they will leave $30 trillion in assets to their children and grandchildren.[36]

Millennials do not have a warm fuzzy feeling toward the stock market; 70 percent keep their savings in cash and avoid investing in mutual funds and other stock market instruments.[37] And, according to a Goldman Sachs survey, they "are more likely to accept a lower return or a higher risk related to an investment if it is in a company that has a positive impact on society and the environment, while less likely to invest in a company that has a negative impact on society and the environment despite potentially large monetary returns."[38]

The upcoming generation is looking for investment opportunities outside of the stock market that provide great values alignment. Up until now, there have not been many companies providing those investment opportunities. If you offer an opportunity like that by following the steps in this book, you may find yourself overwhelmed with potential investors beating down your door!

YOU ARE PART OF A SMALL BUT GROWING MOVEMENT

You are part of a growing movement that is still relatively small. This is the movement of mission-driven entrepreneurs who refuse to try to fit themselves into a mold that doesn't feel aligned with their deepest values. My past clients, such as People's Community Market and Equal Exchange, have been true pioneers—daring to design offerings that were unlike anything that had been done before. Their success stories make it possible for a growing number of entrepreneurs to boldly declare, *I want to do this my way on my own terms.*

Entrepreneurs are some of the most creative and innovative people on the planet, so why should they accept a standardized, cookie-cutter funding model? Especially if this model forces them to sacrifice the very reasons they started their businesses in the first place.

Being at the beginning of a movement is not easy: there will be lots people who think you are crazy. Remember that almost every pioneer is laughed at in the beginning. Eventually, this way of raising capital will be the norm, and no one will remember that it ever wasn't.

There is nothing more important than for you to live your dream and create a business that you love. Go out and get the capital you need to make it happen.

NOTES

1. Antony Page and Robert A. Katz, "Freezing Out Ben & Jerry: Corporate Law and the Sale of a Social Enterprise Icon," *Vermont Law Review* 35 (2010): 219–221, http://ssrn.com/abstract=1724940.
2. Ibid., 218–219.
3. Antony Page and Robert A. Katz, "The Truth About Ben and Jerry's," Stanford *Social Innovation Review*, Fall 2012, https://ssir.org/articles/entry/the_truth_about_ben_and_jerrys.
4. "Raspberry Rebels," *The Economist*, September 4, 1997, www.economist.com/node/156042.
5. James G. Steiker, "Some Real 'Truth' about Ben & Jerry's: A Lawyer's Perspective," *CSRWire Talkback*, October 1, 2012, www.csrwire.com/blog/posts/560-some-real-truth-about-ben-jerrys-a-lawyer-s-perspective.
6. Brad Edmondson, *Ice Cream Social: The Struggle for the Soul of Ben & Jerry's* (San Francisco, CA: Berrett-Koehler, 2014), 4.
7. "Despite Improved Access to Capital, Small Businesses Still Heavily Dependent on Personal Resources, According to Private Capital," *Pepperdine Newsroom*, June 20, 2016, http://newsroom.pepperdine.edu/bschool/2016/06/despite-improved-access-capital-small-businesses-still-heavily-dependent-personal.
8. "Crowdfunding Statistics," *Fundable* (n.d.), www.fundable.com/crowdfunding101/crowdfunding-statistics.
9. Dorie Clark, *Stand Out* (New York, NY: Penguin, 2015), 19.
10. Kate Poole, interview with the author, March 23, 2016.

11. Amy Cortese, *Locavesting* (Hoboken, NJ: John Wiley & Sons, 2011), 21.

12. Securities and Exchange Commission, *Report on the Review of the Definition of "Accredited Investor,"* December 18, 2015, www.sec.gov/corpfin/reportspubs/special-studies/review-definition-of-accredited-investor-12–18–2015.pdf, 48.

13. "SVN Courageous Conversation with Greg Steltenpohl of Califia Farms and Founder of Odwalla," YouTube (May 6, 2013), www.youtube.com/watch?v=LaqIMQHMPoo.

14. Aner Ben-Ami, "Square Peg, Round Hole: Innovating Finance for Social Enterprises," *Transform Finance,* July 26, 2015, http://transformfinance.org/blog/2015/7/26/square-peg-round-hole-innovating-finance-for-social-enterprises.

15. Aner Ben-Ami, "Alternative Deal Structures to Maximize Impact: The Fund Perspective" [Webinar] sponsored by Transform Finance Investor Network, September 29, 2016.

16. Aner Ben-Ami, e-mail message to the author, March 18, 2017.

17. Jonathan Nelson, phone interview with the author, December 16, 2016.

18. Blair Enns, "A Mission with No Exit," Win without Pitching, n.d., www.winwithoutpitching.com/no-exit/.

19. J. D. Harrison, "No, Entrepreneurs, Most of You Don't Need Angel Investors or Venture Capitalists," *Washington Post,* March 16, 2015, www.washingtonpost.com/news/on-small-business/wp/2015/03/16/no-entrepreneurs-most-of-you-dont-need-angel-investors-or-venture-capitalists/?utm_term=.73b1274a24fb.

20. From speech at Social Venture Network conference—April 26, 2013, San Diego, CA.

21. Diane Mulcahy, "Six Myths about Venture Capitalists," *Harvard Business Review,* May 2013, https://hbr.org/2013/05/six-myths-about-venture-capitalists.

22. Angel Capital Association, "FAQs for Angels and Entrepreneurs," n.d., www.angelcapitalassociation.org/faqs/.

23. Ibid.

24. National Venture Capital Association, "2016 Yearbook," 2016, http://nvca.org/pressreleases/2016-nvca-yearbook-captures-busy-year-for-venture-capital-activity/.

25. American Investment Council, "Private Equity: Top States and Districts," www.investmentcouncil.org/private-equity-at-work/education/private-equity-top-states-districts/.

26. Marv Pollack, "How Many Family Offices Are There in the United States?," www.familyoffice.com/insights/how-many-family-offices-are-there-united-states.

27. Investment Company Institute, "2016 Investment Company Fact Book," 2016, www.ici.org/pdf/2016_factbook.pdf.

28. Ibid.

29. Justin McCarthy, "Just over Half of Americans Own Stocks, Matching Record Low," Gallup, April 20, 2016, www.gallup.com/poll/190883/half-americans-own-stocks-matching-record-low.aspx.

30. Lisa Mastny, "Can Investing Locally Give Us a Better Return on Our Money?," *New Dream*, June 21, 2012, www.newdream.org/blog/local-dollars-local-sense.

31. David Gitlin, "Structured Exits: A New Universe of Potential Funding for Companies in Underserved Markets," TheDeal.com, 2015, www.gtlaw.com/News-Events/Publications/Published-Articles/187859/Structured-Exits-A-New-Universe-of-Potential-Funding-for-Companies-in-Undeserved-Markets.

32. Noha Waibsnaider, e-mail message to the author, March 7, 2017.

33. Janie Hoffman, interview with the author, March 11, 2017.

34. Meir Statman, "How Your Emotions Get in the Way of Smart Investing," *Wall Street Journal*, June 14, 2015, www.wsj.com

/articles/how-your-emotions-get-in-the-way-of-smart
-investing-1434046156.

35. Jackie VanderBrug, "Aligning Your Investments with Your
Values," *Capital Acumen*, Summer 2014, www.ustrust.com
/publish/ust/capitalacumen/summer2014/insights/invest
ments-values.html. (This article is no longer available.)

36. Jorge Newbery, "Can Millennials, Crowdfunding, and Impact Investing Change the World?," *Huffington Post*, March 10, 2017,
www.huffingtonpost.com/entry/can-millennials-crowdfunding
-and-impact-investing_us_58c2bd6de4b070e55af9ede1.

37. BlackRock Investor Pulse, "Millennials and Money," 2016,
www.blackrockinvestorpulse.com/millennials.

38. Goldman Sachs, *The Future of Finance*, March 13, 2015,
http://docplayer.net/6624556-The-future-of-finance.html.

GLOSSARY

Accredited investor. Generally, an individual with at least $1 million in net worth excluding his or her home, or $200,000 in annual income; or an organization with at least $5 million in assets. The complete definition can be found in Rule 501 of Regulation D of the 1933 Securities Act (17 CFR 230.501).

Bootstrapping. Starting, running, or growing your business using your personal resources and without external help or capital.

Breakeven. The point at which your company's revenues are enough to cover your expenses.

Due diligence. An examination of relevant documents, facts, assets, and other information about an issuer to help with the decision of whether to invest.

Exit strategy. A strategy or plan for how an investor eventually will get her investment back. A company founder can also have an exit strategy for how she will eventually leave her business.

Form D. A federal form that is filed with the Securities and Exchange Commission to report a sale of securities that is exempt from the federal registration requirement. The form is filed using an online platform called EDGAR (Electronic Data Gathering, Analysis, and Retrieval).

Impact investing. Investing done with the intention of creating a beneficial social or environmental impact in addition to a financial return.

Investment crowdfunding. Another name for a public offering.

Issuer. In a securities offering, the organization whose securities are being offered. For example, if an investor buys shares of Company X, Company X is the issuer of those shares.

Pass-through. A type of taxation in which all tax items (income, loss, deduction, or credit) are passed through to the company owners and reported on their individual tax returns. When a company is taxed as a pass-through, the company itself is not subject to federal tax; the tax obligations are passed through to the company owners.

Private offering (or private placement). A securities offering that is conducted without doing any public advertising. It is generally offered via one-on-one conversations with potential investors.

Pro rata. A way to allocate proportionately. Each investor's pro rata share generally equals the value of that investor's investment divided by the total value of all investments.

Public offering. A securities offering that is made using public advertising.

Safe harbor. When a law is not specific enough to provide clear guidance on how to comply with it, legislators or regulators may create a safe harbor, which is a list of specific requirements that, if met, are deemed to meet the requirements of the law. For example, Section 4(a)(2) of the 1933 Securities Act provides an exemption from the registration requirements for "transactions by an issuer not involving any public offering." Because this exemption is so vague, Rule 506(b) was promulgated to provide detailed requirements that, if met, ensure compliance with Section 4(a)(2). It is possible to comply with Section 4(a)(2) without meeting the requirements of the safe harbor, but meeting the requirements of the safe harbor provides more certainty of compliance, making costly litigation less likely.

Securities offerings. When someone offers to sell securities to someone else. This can be done in a one-on-one conversation or via public advertising.

READERS' RESOURCES WEBSITE

As I've mentioned throughout the book, additional resources for readers are available at jennykassan.com/book resources. The website includes

+ Capital raising success stories
+ Legal developments
+ Sample investor presentation materials from companies that have successfully raised funding
+ Templates for financial projections, valuations, term sheets, and so on
+ Other resources to help you successfully raise capital on your own terms

Because I spend most of my waking hours working with clients to help them raise capital, investing my own money, and connecting with other investors and entrepreneurs, I am constantly learning about tools, strategies, and resources for creative capital raising. The readers' resources website is where I will share this information.

ASSESSMENTS

ARE YOU READY TO RAISE CAPITAL?

I have been working with entrepreneurs to raise capital for about ten years, and I have noticed that those who are successful have certain characteristics in common. I designed this assessment to help you determine whether you have the necessary prerequisites for capital raising success.

1. Are you passionate about your business? When someone asks you about it, do you find yourself lighting up and feeling excited to talk about it?

2. Are you fully committed to being an entrepreneur (i.e., your business is not just a hobby or side project)?

3. Do you feel that what you are trying to achieve with your business is something that you are called to do and that allows you to express your unique genius? Do you feel that this business is something that you can't *not* do?

4. Do you have an interesting story behind your business that you love to tell and that you notice that people love to listen to?

5. Do you believe that you and your family and others close to you will benefit from the success of your business (e.g., you will have more wealth, more free time to travel, growth and learning opportunities, opportunities to contribute to a community you care about)?

6. Are you clear about your core values (i.e., those things that you would not compromise on in your business no matter what)?
7. Do you know who your ideal customers or clients are? Do you have a strategy for reaching them?
8. Answer the question here that applies to your situation:
    a. If you haven't yet started earning revenue, do you know where your revenue will come from? Do you have a clear idea of how much of your products or services you'll have to sell to create a sustainable business?
    b. If you are already earning revenue, are you keeping accurate financial records so that you can see how things are going?
9. Do you know who your competitors are and what makes you different from them?
10. Do you have a vision for the future of your business? In other words, do you have a clear picture of what you would like it to be when it has reached its ideal size (however you define that)?
11. Do you have a sense of your long-term plans for your business? For example, what happens when you're ready to retire? Would you sell the business? Would you leave it to your kids? Would you like to be a serial entrepreneur who sells her first business and then moves on to another one? Or do you want to keep running the business until your last day on earth?

Scoring: Give yourself one point for each yes answer. The higher your score, the more ready you are to raise investment capital.

CAPITAL RAISING DECISION TOOL

This decision tool is designed to help you think through the various components of the instrument you will offer to your investors. It should be used in conjunction with step 3 of part 2 of this book.

1. Given your current financial position and your plans for future financing, is it appropriate and desirable for you to incur debt?

☐   Yes   ☐   No

Explain: _____
_____
_____
_____

If you already have a lot of debt on your books or you plan to apply for institutional financing in the near future, offering a debt security to investors could overload your balance sheet too heavily with debt, making future loans difficult to obtain.

2. Given your realistic financial projections, can you afford and/or do you want to pay a portion of your net revenues to investors (in the form of a distribution, dividend, or interest payment)? If so, how much? Starting in what year?

Explain: _____
_____
_____
_____

If you can afford to pay a regular payment to investors in the form of a dividend, distribution, or interest payment, this can be attractive for investors.

2a. If you do make regular payments to your investors, do you want those to be guaranteed or at your discretion?

Explain: _____

_____

_____

_____

Payments to equity investors can be at your discretion or guaranteed (assuming the company can legally pay—distributions to equity investors can generally be paid only when the company is solvent). Payments on debt must be paid according to the terms of the promissory note. So if you want the flexibility of not having to make a payment to investors, equity is a better option. But note that payments to lenders can be set up to be variable depending on various factors, such as gross revenues—for example, the promissory note could say that the borrower pays the lender 0.1 percent of gross revenues each year.

2b. If the company does very well over the next few years, do you want your investors to benefit from that by getting a higher return on their investment (i.e., do you want them to get a return that varies based on the success of the company as opposed to a fixed return)?

☐   Yes   ☐   No

Explain: _____
_____
_____
_____

If you answer yes to this question, you can offer a debt instrument whose payment varies based on the company's performance, or you can offer equity and pay dividends or distributions based on the performance of the company. With equity, the investors can also participate in the proceeds if the company is sold.

3. Given your realistic financial projections, how do you envision your investors ultimately exiting from their investment?

☐ Investors are paid back their original investment amount out of company funds.
☐ Investors are paid back their original investment amount plus some additional amount out of company funds.
☐ Investors are paid back from proceeds of the sale of the company.
☐ Investors are paid back from proceeds of another securities offering.
☐ Investors sell their security to someone else.
☐ I expect our investors to keep their money in the company indefinitely.
☐ Other: _____
_____
_____
_____

Exit is an important consideration when offering an investment opportunity. The exit from a debt investment happens at the maturity date when the principal is due. The exit from an equity investment can happen in many different ways, and it is best to decide in advance how you want this to work. You can include provisions in your equity instrument—for example, the investor has the right to get 1.5 times the amount originally invested back after ten years, or the investor receives 95 percent of distributable cash until the original investment amount has been recovered and thereafter receives 50 percent of distributable cash. The options are pretty much unlimited. If exit is not addressed in the equity instrument, it usually happens via a sale of the company or the sale of the equity by the investor to another investor.

3a. Do you want your investors to have the right to get their original investment back out at some point, or would you rather they take more risk—that is, have their ability to get paid back depend on the company's performance?

Explain: _____

_____

_____

_____

If you do not want your investors to have the right to get their original investment back, you should offer equity and not debt, as a fundamental characteristic of debt is that the investor has the right to get the original investment (principal) back at the maturity of the loan.

4. Do you want your regular payments to your investors (if any) to be tax deductible to the company?

☐ Yes   ☐ No

Explain: _____

_____

_____

_____

Payments of distributions/dividends to equity investors are not tax deductible to the company, whereas payments of interest to lenders are. So, from the company's perspective, debt is preferable to equity for tax reasons.

5. Do you think your investors will be concerned about the tax treatment of the return on their investment?

☐ Yes   ☐ No

Explain: _____

_____

_____

_____

Dividend payments are often taxed at a lower rate than interest payments on the investor's tax return. So, from the investor's perspective, equity can be preferable. If the entity is treated as a pass-through for tax purposes (generally partnerships, LLCs, and S Corps), equity investors must be provided with a K-1 after the end of each tax year, which tells the investor how the profits or losses of the company must be included on the investor's personal tax return. Tax issues can be quite complicated and vary a lot depending on your particular circumstances. It is best to consult a tax specialist about these issues.

6. Do you want your investors to have any involvement in management (e.g., the right to elect someone to the board, the right to participate in board elections on an equal footing with the company principals, the right to veto certain major decisions)?

☐ Yes   ☐ No

Explain: _____
_____
_____
_____

Lenders usually have no voting rights. Equity investors may have voting rights, which can be structured in many different ways. It is possible to offer an equity instrument that has no voting rights, but the law may still provide for voting rights in special circumstances to protect the investors.

7. Do you want the securities you offer to be convertible into another kind of security at some later date (e.g., the right for your investors to convert their loan into preferred stock if you sell preferred stock to future investors)?

☐ Yes   ☐ No

Explain: _____
_____
_____
_____

Some companies offer debt instruments that are just like a regular loan except that a certain event could trigger the optional or mandatory conversion of the note into equity. The trigger is usually an equity financing round of a certain size. If the trigger doesn't occur before the maturity of the note, the principal and interest generally must be paid to the investor as described in the note.

8. Do you have any thoughts about future fundraising plans that might affect what kind of security you offer now?

☐ Yes ☐ No

Explain: _____

_____

_____

_____

If you plan to raise equity in the future, it is important to carefully structure your current equity round so that it doesn't make a future raise too challenging. One way to ensure greater flexibility is to include a provision that gives you the right to buy equity back from your investors at a pre-agreed price. As mentioned earlier, a debt offering can affect your ability to raise additional funds in the future if the liabilities on your balance sheet become too large for investors' or institutional lenders' comfort.

9. If the company were to dissolve or be sold, would you want your investors to get first dibs on distributions?

☐ Yes ☐ No

raise capital on your own terms

Explain: _____
_____
_____
_____

If you are offering debt, your investors will automatically get first dibs upon dissolution (before the equity holders). If you're offering equity, it's up to you to specify this in something called a *liquidation preference*, which is the investors' right to get paid back before the founders/principals in the case of a liquidation (dissolution or sale). A liquidation preference is a common feature of preferred stock.

The most common approach is to provide a preference equal to the purchase price, but the preference could be greater than or less than that amount.

With "participating" preferred stock, preferred holders are entitled to receive their preference amount first in a liquidation event (plus accrued and unpaid dividends), with any remaining proceeds being divided pro rata among holders of common stock and preferred stock. Professional investors will often demand participation rights. There may be a cap on the participation rights—for example, it may be two times the original investment amount. Preferred stock may be convertible at the election of the holder into common stock at a specified conversion rate (usually initially 1:1, but the rate may adjust over time). Because common shares receive the residual amount in connection with any liquidation (after payment of any liquidation preference to the preferred), the ability of preferred shares to convert to common enables the preferred shares to participate in any

210

upside in the event the liquidation amount exceeds the liquidation preference.

10. Do you want to have the right to buy your investors out (i.e., redeem their investment)?

☐ Yes   ☐ No

Explain: _____

_____

_____

_____

As noted earlier, this can be a good idea to create greater flexibility. In the case of equity, this is called *redemption rights* or a *call option*. In the case of debt, this is called a *prepayment option*.

10a. If so, when and at what price?

_____

_____

In the case of debt, the price will generally be the principal plus any accrued but unpaid interest. You can also offer an additional payment to compensate for the investors' not being able to hold the investment for as long as planned. In the case of equity, the redemption price can be set at the original investment amount or some multiple of that, or can be based on a valuation of the company at the time of redemption.

11. Do you want your investors to be able to transfer their securities to someone else (e.g., to their heirs if they die, to their family members, to anyone?)

☐ Yes   ☐ No

Explain: _____

_____

_____

_____

Some companies choose to limit their investors' right to sell their securities to someone else. This can be done through restrictions on transfer, such as a right of first refusal. Even if your investors have the right to sell to someone else, this can be limited by state or federal securities law and by the difficulty of finding a willing purchaser.

12. How much capacity do you have to prepare accounting documents for your investors (e.g., K-1s)?

Explain: _____

_____

_____

_____

As noted earlier, a pass-through entity requires the preparation of K-1s for equity investors. In other situations, you may be required to provide 1099s to your investors (e.g., if you pay a dividend or interest). You should make sure that you have the capacity to prepare these documents in a timely manner for your investors. They will not be happy if you wait until the last minute, which delays their ability to complete their personal tax returns.

13. Do you want to offer any of the following protections to your investors?

Sinking fund

This means that you promise to regularly set aside money in a separate account for the exclusive purpose of meeting your obligations to your investors. For example, if you promise your investors that you will be able to pay them back their original investment in five years, you would set aside funds regularly to ensure that you have enough money to pay them back when you promised.

☐ Yes   ☐ No

Explain: _____

_____

_____

_____

Pledge regarding liens on the company's property

This is a promise not to enter into financing arrangements that would result in liens on the company's property.

☐ Yes   ☐ No

Explain: _____

_____

_____

_____

Pledge regarding other obligations

This is a promise not to incur any additional debt (or any additional debt in excess of a certain amount or that is not subordinated) until the current investors have been paid.

☐ Yes   ☐ No

Explain: _____

_____

_____

_____

Pledge regarding profit distributions to company principals

This is a promise not to pay any profit distributions to the company principals until the investors have been paid. Of course this does not prevent payment of reasonable salaries.

☐ Yes   ☐ No

Explain: _____

_____

_____

_____

Protective provisions

These are special approval rights with respect to matters of particular significance, such as new financings, payment of distributions, charter or bylaw amendments, and the like.

☐ Yes   ☐ No

Explain: _____
_____
_____
_____

Right of first refusal for future raises

This is the right to participate in future financings, so that investors can maintain their percentage of ownership.

☐ Yes   ☐ No

Explain: _____
_____
_____
_____

Vesting of founders' shares

This is a provision that incentivizes the founders to stay at the company by ensuring that their stock is not fully owned by them unless they stay with the company for a period of time.

☐ Yes   ☐ No

Explain: _____
_____
_____
_____

The options listed in this question are some of the ways you can provide further protection for your investors.

Information rights

These are rights of your investors to receive certain information about the company (e.g., an annual financial report).

☐　Yes　　☐　No

Explain: _____

_____

_____

_____

Equity investors generally have statutory rights to receive certain information. You can offer additional rights if you choose.

Any other protections for investors?

_____

_____

14. Do you want to offer more than one type of security in your securities offering (e.g., give the investors the choice of investing in equity or debt)?

☐　Yes　　☐　No

Explain: _____

_____

_____

_____

Offering more than one type of security can help attract more investors, but it does add complication that can result in additional legal fees and record-keeping requirements.

15. Do you want to offer warrants to your investors?

Warrants provide an option to purchase equity at a particular price (the exercise price) within a set period. Warrants are valuable only to the extent that the value of the company increases in relation to the exercise price. Warrants can be offered as an extra "sweetener" along with a debt or convertible debt offering.

☐ Yes   ☐ No

Explain: _____

_____

_____

_____

16. Do you want to offer perks to investors, such as an invitation to a special event, discount cards, or membership in an exclusive club?

☐ Yes   ☐ No

Explain: _____

_____

_____

_____

Perks can make an investment opportunity more attractive by making investors feel special and part of a community.

INDEX

accredited investors: angel investors considered to be, 16–18, 53; as defined under federal securities law, 29; demographics of, 54; legal compliance strategies and, 29–30; professional investors as, 4–5, 53, 54; Rule 506(b) on private offerings to, 120, 121, 122, 123, 124, 146, 152; venture capitalist (VCs) as, 16–18, 40–42, 52–53. *See also* investors

"active angels," 53

advertising public securities offerings: potential hazards of, 118–19; Rule 504 on state registration allowing, 127–29

agricultural co-cops, 141–42

Angel Capital Association, 53

angel investors: "active angels" considered to be professional investors, 53; capital raising myths and truths to remember, 16–18; description of, 53; financial return expectations of, 17; pitch deck to present to, 154–55; Rule 506(b) on private offerings to, 120, 121, 122, 123, 124, 146, 152. *See also* investor types

anti-dilution protection, 109

Articles of Organization, 72

authenticity, 161–62

baby boomer assets, 189

Ben-Ami, Aner, 40–41

benefit corporations, 69–70

Ben & Jerry's Homemade Ice Cream: cautionary tale of raising funds by, 2–3; professional investors pushing them to sell, 3, 5

Bioneers, 159, 186

bond investments, 54, 55

bootstrapping: description of, 20; when it is time to stop, 20–22

breakeven point, 47

Buffett, Warren, 170

business/companies: community or tribe connected to your, 163; financial projections for, 45–47; funding and risk of losing control of your, 2–3, 5, 17, 18; identifying your *why* for, 36–37, 176; "lifestyle business" model of, 169; pledge regarding liens on property of, 110; pledge regarding other obligations of, 110; pledge regarding profit distributions to principals of, 110; risk of investment in, 169–71; sale of the, 16, 107–8, 168–69; up-front investment for, 45–46; when to stop bootstrapping the funding of your, 20–22; your values and goals for your, 7–9, 33–40; your vision of your, 37–38; "zombie," 42

business control: Ben & Jerry's Homemade Ice Cream cautionary tale on losing, 2–3, 5; convertible notes and the possibility of losing, 97–98; Greg Steltenpohl's story on losing Odwalla, Inc., 33–34; it is possible to raise capital without losing, 18; myth on advantages of giving investors the, 17; venture capitalist expectations for, 57. *See also* entrepreneur founders

business decisions: choosing an instrument, 65, 76–85; decision tree on legal compliance strategy for, 147; economic rights, 65, 85–111; figuring how much

business decisions (*continued*)
money you need to raise, 44–50; never
make one at the expense of your values
and goals, 36–37. *See also* decision
making rights; governance rights
business goals. *See* goals

capital raising: busting some of the
common myths about, 16–17; common
fears and doubts related to, 24, 175;
devoting the time necessary for successful,
188–89; establishing how much money
you need, 44–50; getting ready to get
serious about, 23–24; misinformation
and confusion about, 13–16; Nina
Simons on "cultivating garden" analogy
for, 186; six steps for plan on, 7–11; true
statements about, 17–18; what your
lawyer won't tell you about securities
laws, 25–32. *See also* funding; venture
capital (VC) model
Capital Raising Decision Tool, 116
capital raising goals: figuring out how much
you need, 44–45; financial projections
approach to calculating amount, 45–47;
needed equipment and purchases to
calculate amount, 47–49; raising more
than one round to meet your, 49–50
capital raising myths: on advantage of
delaying equity to, 17; on advantages of
giving investor's control, 17; investors
always set the terms of investment, 17;
on "liquidity event" as only way for
raising funds quickly, 16; that raising
funds means giving up control, 17; that
you must always put investors' interests
first, 17; that you need to tailor your
business to fit investor expectations, 17
capital raising plans: step 1: get clear on
your goals and values, 7–9, 33–50, 187;
step 2: identify the right investors for
you, 9, 51–62, 187; step 3: design your
offer, 9–10, 63–116, 187–88; step 4:
choose your legal compliance strategy,
10, 117–47, 188; step 5: enroll investors,
10–11, 148–74, 188; step 6: address

obstacles head on, 11, 175–86, 188. *See
also* entrepreneur founders
capital raising truths: a company can be
designed to reduce investor lawsuits,
18; on financial return expectations of
investors, 17–18, 52–53; it is possible to
raise capital without giving up control,
18; liquidity event as unnecessary to pay
back investors, 18; remember that each
investor is unique, 18; that the "smart
money" doesn't always make best
decision, 18; you can design any type of
investment offering, 18
C Corps: preferred stock of, 100; taxation
of, 70, 73
CERO Cooperative, 45
Certificate of Formation, 72
Clark, Dorie, 14–15
Coca-Cola, 33
Cohen, Ben, 2, 3
common stock, 69, 112
community: impact investing concerns with
impact on, 5; Kate Poole as investor
interesting in contributing to, 18–19;
non-financial benefits of investment
related to, 171–73; tied to your business,
163
companies. *See* business/companies
compensation. *See* equity investor
compensation
compliance. *See* legal compliance strategy;
securities laws
control. *See* business control
conversion rights, 109
convertible debt (or convertible promissory
notes): additional variations that can be
included in, 96–97; basic provisions of a
simple, 94–96; caution about possibility
of losing business control with, 97–98;
description of, 80, 82–83; including
"most favored nation" status in, 97;
as usually advised by lawyers, 63
convertible equity, 84
co-ops (cooperatives): compliance of
securities offers by agricultural, 141–42;
description and considerations for,

73–74; limited cooperative association (LCA) type of, 74; selecting Subchapter T or Subchapter K tax status of, 74

corporations: benefit corporations and social purpose corporations, 69–70; as independent legal entity, 68; limited liability of, 67; nonprofit organizations, 31, 74–75; shares of stock ownership of, 68–69; taxation as C Corps, 66, 70; taxation as S Corps, 66, 70–72, 100

co-sale rights, 109

crowdfunding: avoiding security compliance through, 27; Indiegogo platform for, 26; JOBS ACT Title III on registration exemptions to, 126, 131–39, 150; Kickstarter platform for, 4, 26; newbie investor questions about, 166–67; raising funds through, 4

"cultivating a garden" analogy, 186

cumulative distributions, 101–2

data collection: field work for gathering investor, 60; sample scripts to use for gathering investor, 60–62

debt instruments: convertible promissory note or convertible, 82–83; deciding on equity versus, 76; decision-making rights in, 112; promissory notes as evidence of, 27, 77; tax implications of, 78; understanding what it is, 77–78

debt investor economic rights: information rights, 111; pledge regarding liens on the company's property, 110; pledge regarding other obligations, 110; pledge regarding profit distributions to company principals, 110; security interest, 111; vesting of founders' shares, 110–11

debt offering examples: Farm Fresh to You, 93; The Force for Good Fund, 93–94; Red Bay Coffee, 94

debt offerings: higher interest rates, 91; letting investors participate in a pay payday, 92–93; performance-based models, 88–90; simple models, 86–87; staggered maturity, 91–92; three

examples of creative, 93–94; zero-interest loans, 91

decision making rights: in debt instruments, 112; in equity instruments, 112–13; typically requested by VCs, 113. See also business decisions

depository accounts investments, 54

distributions. See profit distributions

dividends: as corporate payment to shareholders, 99–100; "double tax" of entity level and also, 70; generally lower taxes on, 81; as negating need for liquidity event, 99; People's Community Market example of, 102; Subchapter K pass-through treatment of LLC, 73; Subchapter T beneficial tax treatment of, 74; taxes paid on their pro rata share of, 71

Dow Jones Industrial Average annual return, 168

due diligence, 151

economic rights: deciding your investor, 65, 111; offered to both equity and debt investors, 110–11; offered to equity investors, 108–9

The Economist, 3

employees: caution against using unpaid interns, 46–47; financial projections for, 46–49

employment law, 46–47

Enns, Blair, 42

entrepreneur founders: be authentic, 161–62; Ben & Jerry's story on losing control of their business, 2–3, 5; capital raising myths and truths for, 16–18; common capital raising fears and doubts of, 24; common stock issued to, 69; convertible notes and the possibility of losing control by, 97–98; fear that they can't provide a 30x return, 176–77; goals and values of, 7–9, 33–50; numerous barriers faced by, 1; offering equity investors a preference to profits before the, 100; overcoming obstacles exercises for, 180–85; remember mutual need of

entrepreneur founders (*continued*)
investors and, 180; risks of raising
funding for, 2–3; share what makes
you special, 162–63; share your vision,
160–61; taking care of yourself, 185;
vesting of founders' shares, 110–11; when
to stop bootstrapping your business,
20–22; where to find the right funding,
3–6. *See also* business control; capital
raising plans

entrepreneur founders–investor relationship:
different options for kinds of, 58;
importance of cultivating the, 57–58

environmental impact: impact investing
concerns with, 5; Kate Poole as investor
interesting in contributing to, 18–19;
as non-financial benefits of investment,
171–73

Equal Exchange, 105–6, 113, 179, 190

equipment: exercise for identifying what
you need and costs for, 47–49; up-front
investment required for, 45–46

equity: deciding on debt versus, 76;
understanding what it is, 78–80;
valuation of, 102–3. *See also* equity
investor compensation

equity economic rights: anti-dilution
protection, 109; conversion rights, 109;
information rights, 111; pledge regarding
liens on company's property, 110; pledge
regarding other obligations, 110;
pledge regarding profit distributions to
company principals, 110; preemptive
rights, 109; registration rights, 109; right
of first refusal and co-sale rights, 109;
security interest for debt investors, 111;
vesting of founders' shares, 110–11

equity instruments: convertible, 84;
decision-making rights in, 112–13;
economic rights offered to investors,
108–11; liquidity event for exit or sale
of, 16, 18, 99, 103–8, 142–43, 168–69;
redemption (or put), 104, 105–7; SAFE
(simple agreement for future equity),
83–84; sale to third party, 105. *See also*
instruments; taxation

equity investor compensation: cumulative
versus noncumulative distributions,
101–2; dividends, 70–71, 73–74, 81,
99–100, 102; liquidity event for exit or
sale of, 16, 18, 99, 103–8, 142–43,
168–69; a note about valuation,
102–3; profit distributions, 98–101;
redemption, 105–7; sale of equity to a
third party, 105; 30x return for, 176–77.
See also equity; investors; liquidity
events

executive summary document, 153–54

expenses: associated with employment,
46–49; exercise for identifying
equipment, 47–49; up-front investment
required, 45–46. *See also* financial
projections

Farm Fresh to You, 93

Fast Company magazine, 19

federal registration: initial public offering
(IPO) with SEC, 28–29; JOBS Act
Title III crowdfunding exemption, 126,
131–39, 150; Regulation S safe-harbor
exemption for offerings outside the US,
142–43. *See also* state registration

federal rules: Rule 504 (up to $5 million),
121–22, 127–29; Rule 506(b) [accredited
investors only], 120, 121, 122, 123, 124,
146, 152. *See also* securities laws

field work: collecting investor data through,
60; sample scripts to use for, 60–62

financial projections: calculating your
capital raising amount using, 45–47;
description and benefits of, 45;
estimating your breakeven point, 47;
template to use for, 46. *See also* expenses

finders: considering pros and cons of using,
174; description and resources for,
173

FINDRA, 173

following up investor meeting, 173

The Force for Good Fund, 93–94

Form 1099-INT, 78

Form D [for Rule 506(b)], 120, 122, 152

founders. *See* entrepreneur founders

funding: Ben & Jerry's Homemade Ice Cream
cautionary story on raising, 2–3; tapping
the most abundant source of, 6–11;
understanding the risks for entrepreneurs,
2–3; when to stop bootstrapping your
business, 20–22; where to find the right,
3–6. See also capital raising

funding sources: capital raising plan to tap,
6–11; considering other alternatives for,
5–6; crowdfunding and Kickstarter
campaigns, 4; professional investors, 4–5

fund managers, 53

fundraising. See capital raising

Gather Restaurant (Berkeley), 101

goals: calculating capital raising, 44–49;
don't sacrifice them for the venture
capital (VC) model, 43–44; get clear
on your, 7–9; identifying your business,
39–40; identifying your personal, 35–36;
never make a business decision at the
expense of your, 36–37; nonnegotiable,
38–39; risk of raising capital at the
sacrifice of your, 33–34; staying on track
by aligning strategy with your, 50; your
why for business, 36–37, 176

Goldin, Kara, 46

Goldman Sachs millennials survey, 190

governance rights: choosing investor, 65,
114; decision-making rights in debt
instruments, 112; decision-making rights
in equity instruments, 112–13; things to
consider when assigning, 114; typically
given to venture capitalists, 113. See also
business decisions

Greenfield, Jerry, 2, 3

Greyston Bakery, 2

Hackers/Founders, 41–42

Hint Water, 46

Hoffman, Janie, 165

ideal investors: creating a profile for your,
56–57; cultivating a relationship with
your, 57–58; doing field work to collect
data on, 60–62; how to find your, 59–60;

identifying your, 9, 56; importance of
narrowing down your choices to, 55;
taking the time to find your, 62

impact investing movement: description
and focus of the, 5; Kate Poole on her
commitment to, 18–19; rejecting the
traditional VC funding model, 190–91

impound accounts, 131

Inc. 500, 42

Indiegogo, 26

information rights, 111

initial public offerings (IPOs): exit or sale
of equity without doing an, 104; as not
the only way for fast business growth,
16; reality of investors losing money
on unsuccessful, 168; registration of
securities with SEC for, 28–29; sale of
investor's equity through, 103. See also
public offerings

instruments: convertible debt or convertible
promissory note, 63, 80, 82–83, 94–98;
convertible equity, 84; debt, 76, 77–78,
86–111, 112; KISS (Keep It Simple
Security), 84; prepayment, 84, 85; SAFE
(simple agreement for future equity),
83–84. See also equity instruments

integration requirements, 144–45

Internal Revenue Code (IRC):
Section 501(c)(3) tax status, 75;
Section 521 tax exemption, 141–42;
Section 25102(e) statute exemption,
15; Subchapter C, 70, 73; Subchapter K,
73, 74; Subchapter S, 66, 70–72, 73,
100; Subchapter T, 73, 74

Internal Revenue Service (IRS) forms:
Form 1099-INT, 78; Form D [for Rule
506(b)], 120, 122, 152

interns: caution against using unpaid,
46–47; petition to SEC requesting
exemption from compliance
requirements from student, 125–26

intrastate exemptions: one state only on
public offerings, 129–30; Rule 147A
on private offerings, 122

investment agreement (or subscription
agreement) document, 151–52

investments: entrepreneur fear that they can't provide a 30x return to, 176–77; investment agreement (or subscription agreement) document on, 151–52; investor desire for alignment of their values and, 177; JOBS Title III exemption for crowdfunding, 126, 131–39, 150; newbie investor questions about, 166–73; non-financial benefits of, 171–73; risk of, 169–71, 177–78

investor enrollment: creating a plan for your, 10–11, 148–49; following up after the meeting, 173; how to ask for meeting with investor, 157–73; a note about using finders, 173–74; special considerations for newbie, 166–73; what to prepare before meeting with investors, 149–57

investor meeting preparation: due diligence process by investors, 151; executive summary document, 153–54; investor questionnaire to give to Rule 506(b) accredited investors, 152; legal requirements to take care of, 150–52; other options for additional, 157; pitch deck slides, 154–55; private placement memorandum (PPM), 156–57; *prospectus* (disclosure documents or offering circular), 128, 150; subscription agreement or investment agreement document, 151–52; term sheet, 156

investor meetings: be authentic, 161–62; be prepared to walk away from the, 165–66; documents and other preparations for, 149–57; following up after the, 173; get a yes or a no by the end of the, 164; how to ask for the, 157–59; make your offer, 163–64; share what makes you special, 162–63; share your vision during the, 160–61; start with questions, 159–60; talk about your community, 163

investors: adding perks for your, 65, 114–15; capital raising plan for enrolling, 10–11; considering other funding options than, 5–6; desire for investment alignment with their values,

177; economic rights of, 65, 108–11; enrolling, 10–11, 148–74; governance rights of, 65, 112–14; growing impact investing movement among, 5, 18–19, 190–91; identifying your ideal, 9, 55–62; millennials as the new generation of, 189–90; myths versus truths about, 16–18; narrowing down the ones to approach, 55–62; non-financial investment benefits to, 171–73, 177; Put Yourself in the Investor's Shoes exercise, 184–85; recognizing the value of your offering to, 176–80; relationship with your, 57–58; remember mutual need of entrepreneurs and, 180; remember that each of them are unique, 18; securities law governing how funds are raising from, 14; special considerations for newbie, 166–73; using finders to locate, 173–74. *See also* accredited investors; equity investor compensation

investor selection: creating your ideal investor profile, 56–57; cultivating a relationship with investors, 57–58; doing field work to collect data on investor, 60–62; how to find your investors, 59–60; identifying your ideal investor, 9, 55–62; importance of narrowing down your, 55; what you don't want in an investor, 57

investor types: the ideal investor, 9, 55–62; nonprofessional, 54–55; professional investors, 4–5, 18–19, 53, 54, 151. *See also* angel investors; venture capitalists (VCs)

investor–founder relationship: different options for kinds of, 58; importance of cultivating the, 57–58

issuer, 78

JOBS (Jumpstart Our Business Startups) ACT: Regulation A+ created under, 126, 139–40, 150; Rule 506(c) created under Title II of, 126, 127; Title III investment crowdfunding exemption, 126, 131–39, 150; Title IV on state level registrations, 139–40

Kahneman, Danny, 115
Kansas securities law (1911), 25
Kick Limiting Beliefs to the Curb exercise,
180–84
Kickstarter campaign, 4, 26
KISS (Keep It Simple Security), 84

lawyers: employment, 47; finalizing your
compliance strategy role of, 147;
finalizing your securities offering role of,
115–16; misinformation and confusion
about capital raising by, 13–15; not
taking the time to learn other funding
pathways, 15–16; what they won't tell
you about securities laws, 25–32. *See also*
securities laws
legal compliance requirements: accredited
investors and, 29–30, 120; federal
registration, 28–29, 126, 131–39,
142–43; including a strategy in capital
raising plan for, 10; JOBS (jumpstart
Our Business Startups) ACT, 126, 127,
131–40; Regulation A and Regulation
A+, 126, 139–40, 150; Section 25102(e)
statute exemption in, 15; state
registration, 25–26, 28–29, 31, 129–31,
139–41; student intern petition to SEC
requesting exemption from, 125–26. *See
also* liquidity events
legal compliance strategy: capital raising
plan inclusion of, 10; consulting a lawyer
to finalize documents on, 147; decision
tree to help choose a, 147; integration of
two offerings, 144–45; legal requirements
before meeting with investors, 150–52;
for private offerings, 120–23, 144–45,
147; for public offerings, 118–19,
126–45, 147; questions to ask for
choosing your, 118; recap of legal
requirements for investment, 117–19;
on resale of securities, 146; on who can
make the offering, 143–44; why public
offerings with advertising increase
expense of, 118–19. *See also* securities
laws
life insurance funds, 55

"lifestyle business" model, 169
limited cooperative association (LCA),
74
limited liability companies (LLCs): Articles
of Organization or Certificate of
Formation to form, 72; common stock
in, 112; limited liability of, 67; offering
memberships in, 27, 72; preferred
memberships or preferred units, 101;
selecting a tax status (Subchapters S, or
K, T) for, 65–66, 73
limited partners (LPs), 52. *See also* venture
capitalists (VCs)
limiting beliefs: damage that is done by,
180–81; Kick Limiting Beliefs to the
Curb exercise to overcome, 180–84;
unconscious thoughts versus rational
thoughts, 182–83
liquidation preference, 107–8
liquidity events: dividends as negating need
for, 99; exit or sale of equity, 103–7;
initial public offering (IPO), 16, 28–29,
103, 104, 168–69; newbie investor
question about receiving money from,
168–69; as not the only way for fast
business growth, 16; Regulation S
(offers/sales outside the US), 142–43;
sale of the company, 16, 107–8, 168–69;
as unnecessary for investors to get paid
back, 18. *See also* legal compliance
requirements

Mamma Chia, 165
market-rate returns, 167–68
millennial investors, 189–90
mind-set adjusting strategies: by recognizing
non-financial investment benefits,
171–73, 177; by remembering investors
and entrepreneurs need one another, 180;
by remembering your *why*, 36–37, 176;
resetting mind-set by recognizing value
of your offering for, 176–80
mind-set adjustment exercises: Kick
Limiting Beliefs to the Curb, 180–84;
Put Yourself in the Investor's Shoes,
184–85; Take Care of Yourself, 185;

mind-set adjustment exercises (*continued*) unconscious thoughts versus rational thoughts, 182–83

mind-set obstacles: capital raising plan addressing head-on the, 11; fears and doubts underlying excuses, 24, 175; numerous ones faced by entrepreneurs, 1; risky investment as entrepreneur, 177–79; risky investment as investor, 169–71

"most favored nation" status, 97

mutual funds investment, 54, 55

negative cash flow, 45–46

Nelson, Jonathan, 41–42

newbie investor questions: on crowdfunding legalities, 166–67; on how they will get their money back, 168–69; on "lifestyle business," 169; on market-rate returns, 167–68; on non-financial benefits of investing, 171–73; on risk of investment, 169–71; on their status as an investor, 167

New York Stock Exchange, 37

Nia House preschool (Berkeley), 31

noncumulative distributions, 101–2

non-financial investment benefits, 171–73, 177

nonnegotiables, 38–39

nonprofessional investors, 54–55

nonprofit organizations: description and considerations of, 74–75; The Force for Good Fund, 93–94; 1933 Securities Act Section 3(a)(4) registration exemption of, 140–41; Section 501(c)(3) tax status of, 75; securities laws on, 31, 140–41

North American Securities Administrators Association (NASAA), 130–31

Obama, Barack, 126

obstacles. *See* mind-set obstacles

Odwalla Inc., 33–34

offerings. *See* securities offerings

Organic Valley, 141

Orsi, Janelle, 125

Our Harvest (Cincinnati), 101

partnerships: as legal entity, 66–67; taxation of, 67

pass-through taxation, 71

Peeled Snacks, 160

pension funds, 54, 55

People's Community Market (Oakland), 102, 179, 190

perks: decision point on adding investor, 65, 114–15; examples of creative investor, 114

"phantom income" problem, 71

Pi Investments, 41

pitch deck, 154–55

preemptive rights, 109

preference: liquidation, 107–8; profits, 100

preferred equity: C Corp preferred stock, 100–1; LLC preferred memberships or units, 101; Our Harvest and Gather Restaurant examples of, 101

prepayment campaign, 84, 85

private equity investors, 53

private offerings compliance strategies: decision tree to help choose your, 147; integration requirements for two, 144–45; resale of securities, 146; Rule 147A on intrastate exemption, 122; Rule 504 up to $5 million, 121–22; Rule 506(b) for accredited investors, 120, 121, 122, 123, 124, 146, 152; Rule 506(b) on accredited investors, 120, 121, 122, 123, 124, 146, 152; Section 4(a)(2) of the 1933 Securities Act, 123; on who can make the offering, 143–44

private offerings (or private placement): integration of two, 144–45; no public advertising or communication about, 119; public versus, 30; resale of securities, 146; various compliance strategies for, 120–23; who can make the offering, 143–44; why compliance strategy is less expensive in, 118–19

private placement memorandum (PPM), 156–57

professional investors: "active angels" included as, 53; demographics of, 54;

description and types of, 4–5, 53; due diligence process by, 151; impact investing movement among some, 5, 18–19, 190–91; Kate Poole's example opposite to stereotypical, 18–19; pushing Ben & Jerry's to sell to highest bidder, 5

profit distributions: cumulative versus noncumulative, 101–2; equity investor compensation through, 98–108; offering equity investors a preference, 100; offering liquidation preference, 108; pledge regarding company principals and, 110; valuation issue, 102–3

promissory notes: convertible, 63, 80, 82–83; debt is evidenced with a, 27, 77

pro rata share tax, 71

prospectus (disclosure documents or offering circular), 128, 150

public benefit corporation statutes, 69–70

public offerings: advantages of, 123–26; advertising of, 118–19; integration of, 144–45; number of investors allowed in, 124–25; private versus, 30; registration rights for, 109; resale of securities, 146; who can make the, 143–44; why compliance strategy is more expensive in, 118–19. *See also* initial public offerings (IPOs)

public offerings compliance strategies: agricultural co-ops and Section 521 tax exemption, 141–42; decision tree to help choose your, 147; federal registration, 28–29, 126, 131–39, 142–43; impound accounts which may be required by states, 131; integration requirements for two offerings, 144–45; JOBS Act Title III federal crowdfunding exemption, 126, 131–39, 150; JOBS Act Title IV on state level registrations, 139–40; NASAA's SCOR form to standardize state registrations, 130–31; nonprofit federal and some states exemptions, 31, 140–41; potential hazards of advertising, 118–19; Regulation S on outside the US offerings, 142–43; resale of securities,

146; Rule 504 on up to $5 million allowing advertising with state compliance, 127–29; Rule 506(c) on accredited investors only, 127; state impound accounts requirements, 131; state-level crowdfunding exemptions, 129–30; state registration, 25–26, 28–29, 31, 128–31, 139–40; on who can make the offering, 143–44

put (or redemption): sale of equity through a, 104; three models for, 105–7

Put Yourself in the Investor's Shoes exercise, 184–85

Real Goods Trading, 105

Red Bay Coffee, 94

redemption (or put): sale of equity through a, 104; three models for, 105–7

redemption (or put) models: Equal Exchange system, 105–6, 113, 179, 190; investor right to redemption, 107; periodic mandatory, 106–7; as structured exits, 107

registration exemptions: agricultural co-ops, 141–42; JOBS Act Title III crowdfunding exemption, 126, 131–39, 150; nonprofit federal and some states, 31, 140–41; public offerings intrastate exemption for one state only, 129–30; Regulation S safe-harbor exemption for offerings outside the US, 142–43; state-level investment crowdfunding exemption, 129–30

registration requirements: initial public offering (IPO) with SEC for federal, 28–29; state securities offerings for individual state, 25–26, 28–29, 31, 128–29

registration rights, 109

Regulation A, 139

Regulation A+ (JOBS Act), 126, 139–40, 150

Regulation S safe-harbor exemption, 142–43

retirement investments, 54, 55

right of first refusal, 109

risk of investment: as obstacle to
entrepreneur, 177–79; as obstacle to
investor, 169–71
RSF Social Finance (California nonprofit),
140–41
Rule 147A (intrastate exemption), 122
Rule 504 (up to $5 million): on private
offerings, 121–22; on public offerings,
127–29
Rule 506(b) [accredited investors only]:
preemption of state laws on, 121, 122;
preparing an investor questionnaire
to accredited investors, 152; private
offerings to accredited investors only,
120; on public offerings, 124; resale of
securities as not automatically exempt
under, 146; safe harbor function of,
123
Rule 506(c): JOBS Act creation of the, 127;
lack of popularity among investors, 127

safe harbor [Rule 506(b)], 123
sale of company: liquidation preference in
case of, 107–8; myth that it is the only
way for investor return, 16; newbie
question on receiving money from,
168–69
S Corps: corporations that are, 70–72;
limited liability companies (LLCs) as,
73; taxation of, 66, 70–72, 100
SCOR (Small Company Offering
Registration) Form [NASAA], 130–31
Section 501(c)(3) [IRC], 75
Section 521 (IRC), 141–42
Section 25102(e) [IRC], 15
securities: description of what it is, 26–28,
117; limited liability company (LLC)
memberships type of, 27, 72; myth on
advantage of delaying an offer to investors,
17; private, 30; promissory notes type of,
27; public, 30, 109
Securities Act (1933): Section 3(a)(4)
registration exemption of public
offerings, 140–41; Section 4(a)(2)
registration exemption of private
offerings, 123

Securities and Exchange Commission
(SEC): integration requirements and
decision of, 144–45; JOBS Act Title IV
(Regulation A+) filing with the, 126,
139–40, 150; process allowing citizens
to submit petitions requesting rule
changes, 125; registration of securities
with the, 28–29, 117–18; Rule 147A on
intrastate exemption updated by the, 122;
Rule 506(c) statistics as reported by, 127;
student intern petition requesting
exemption from registration made to,
125–26
securities laws: on accredited investors,
29–30, 120; on agricultural cooperatives
(co-ops), 141–42; compliance
requirements, 10, 15, 25–26, 28–30, 31;
description of, 10; Dorie Clark's
approach to, 14–15; federal offerings
registration, 28–29, 126, 131–39,
142–43; as governing how businesses
raise money from investors, 14; history
and primary purpose of, 25–26; legal
requirements before meeting with
investors, 150–52; on nonprofit
organizations, 31, 140–41; on public
versus a private offerings, 30; safe harbor
[Rule 506(b)], 123; Section 3(a)(4) of
the Securities Act (1933), 140–41;
Section 4(a)(2) of the Securities Act
(1933), 123; state offerings registration,
25–26, 28–29, 31, 128–31, 139–40; on
third party sale of equity, 105; what your
lawyer won't tell you about, 25–32. See
also federal rules; lawyers; legal
compliance strategy
securities offering decision points: 1:
understand your structure and decide
on the best on, 65–76; 2: choose an
instrument, 65, 76–85; 3: economic
rights, 65, 85–111; 4: governance rights,
65, 111–14; 5: add the perks, 65,
114–15
securities offering design: Capital Raising
Decision Tool, 116; capital raising plan
on, 9–10; choosing a security that fulfills

its promises, 64; convertible note, 63; five decision points while creating your, 64–115; putting it in proper legal form, 115–16; understanding the effects of each particular, 63–64; your ability to create any type of, 18

securities offerings: by agricultural cooperatives (co-ops), 141–42; designing your, 9–10, 18, 63–116; initial public offering (IPO), 16, 28–29, 103–4, 168; integration, 144–45; myth on advantage of delaying an, 17; by nonprofits, 31, 140–41; private (or private placement), 30, 118–23, 143–45, 147; *prospectus* (disclosure documents or offering circular) on, 128, 150; public, 30, 109, 118–19, 123–47; recognizing the value of your, 176–80; registration required for, 25–26, 28–29, 31, 117–19; Regulation S (offers/sales outside the US), 142–43; resale of securities, 146; who can make the, 143–44

securities registration: federal and state, 28–29; nonprofit organizations exempt from, 31; recap of requirements for, 117–19; required for offerings, 25–26

security interest rights, 111

Seeds of Change, 159

shareholders: description of, 68; dividend payments to, 70, 71, 73, 74, 81, 99–102, 102

Shuman, Michael, 55

Sierra Club, 60

Silicon Valley model. *See* venture capital (VC) model

Simons, Nina, 159, 186

sinking fund, 110

social purpose corporations, 69–70

sole proprietorships: as legal entity, 66–67; taxation of, 67

Stand Out (Clark), 14–15

state laws: requiring impound accounts for public offerings, 131; Rule 147A (intrastate exemption) on private offerings, 122; Rule 504 on up to $5 million allowing public offering advertising

with compliance of, 127–29; Rule 506(b) [accredited investors only] preemption of, 120, 121, 122, 123, 124, 146

state registration: investment crowdfunding exemption, 129–30; JOBS Act Title IV (Regulation A+) allowing public offerings without, 126, 139–40, 150; NASAA's SCOR (Small Company Offering Registration) Form for, 130–31; nonprofit exemptions for some states, 31, 140–41; process and requirements for, 25–26, 28–29, 31, 128–29; regional coordinated review for, 131. *See also* federal registration

Steltenpohl, Greg, 33–34

stock: classes of voting and nonvoting, 68–69; common, 69, 112; investment in, 54, 55; ownership shares of, 68–69; preferred, 100–1

stockholders, 68

stock market investment, 54, 55

structured exits, 107

Subchapter C (IRC), 70, 73

Subchapter K (IRC), 73, 74

Subchapter S (IRC): corporations, 70–72; limited liability companies (LLCs), 73; taxation as S Corps, 66, 70–72, 100

Subchapter T (IRC), 73, 74

subscription agreement (or investment agreement) document, 151–52

Sustainable Economies Law Center, 125

Take Care of Yourself exercise, 185

taxation: agricultural co-cops exemption under Section 521, 141, 142; C Corps, 66, 70; debt implications for, 78; implications of equity, 81–82; nonprofit Section 501(c)(3) tax status, 75; pass-through, 71; "phantom income" problem of, 71; pro rata share of profits for dividend, 71; S Corps, 66, 70–72, 100; selecting tax status for corporation, 65–66, 70–72; selecting tax status for LLC, 65–66, 73; sole proprietorships and partnerships, 67. *See also* equity

term sheet, 156

third party equity sale, 105

30x return, 176–77

Thurman, Howard, 21

Tversky, Amos, 115

unconscious thoughts versus rational thoughts exercise, 182–83

Unilever, 3

up-front investment, 45–46

valuation, 102–3

values: don't sacrifice them for the venture capital (VC) model, 43–44; get clear on your, 7–9; identifying your, 34–35; investor desire for investment alignment with their, 177; never make a business decision at the expense of your, 36–37; risk of raising capital at the sacrifice of your, 33–34; staying on track by aligning strategy with your, 50; your nonnegotiables, 38–39; your *why* for business, 36–37, 176

"VC horror stories," 43

venture capitalists (VCs): 30x return (VC-speak for returning thirty time investment), 176–77; business control expectations of, 57; capital raising myths and truths to remember about, 16–18; description of, 52–53; financial return expectations of, 17, 41–42, 52–53; pitch deck to present to, 154–55; preferred stock typically insisted on by, 100–1; Rule 506(b) on private offerings to, 120, 121, 122, 123, 124, 146; typical governance rights requested by, 113. *See also* investor types; limited partners (LPs)

venture capital (VC) model: assumptions of the, 40; don't sacrifice your business goals to, 43–44; equity compensation and economic rights, 98–111; growing awareness of alternatives to the, 40–44; impact investing movement rejecting the, 5, 18–19, 190–91; on liquidity events, 16, 18, 99, 103–4; some truths about, 52; "VC horror stories" associated with the, 43. *See also* capital raising

vesting founders' shares, 110–11

Waibsnaider, Noha, 160

Wall Street Journal, 168, 184

wealth managers, 53

The Win without Pitching Manifesto (Enns), 42

your nonnegotiables, 38–39

your *why*: identifying your, 36–37; overcoming your fears by remembering, 176

"zombie" companies, 42

ABOUT THE AUTHOR

Jenny Kassan has over two decades of experience as an entrepreneur and attorney. She grew up in Los Angeles, but fell in love with the San Francisco Bay Area when she attended UC Berkeley as an undergraduate.

She spent one year between college and law school in Washington, DC, where she worked for Ralph Nader's Center for the Study of Responsive Law and for the Institute for Policy Studies.

Jenny graduated from Yale Law School in 1995 and then moved back to Berkeley with a National Science Foundation fellowship that allowed her to spend three years at UC Berkeley getting a master's degree in city and regional planning with an emphasis on community development.

While in the master's program, Jenny began working at one of the nation's oldest and most respected community development corporations, the Spanish Speaking Unity Council (now the Unity Council), in the Fruitvale neighborhood of Oakland. While there, Jenny served as in-house legal counsel, assisted with the development of the Fruitvale Transit Village, worked on neighborhood commercial district revitalization, and started and ran several social enterprises including a sidewalk cleaning company that is still in operation today.

After eleven years at the Unity Council, Jenny left to join a small boutique law firm led by one of the nation's top securities lawyers, John Katovich, who had served as chief counsel at the Pacific Stock Exchange. That was where Jenny learned about securities law and became passionate about helping mission-driven entrepreneurs raise capital on their own terms.

She and John later cofounded Cutting Edge Capital, a business whose mission is to support social enterprises with their capital raising efforts. Jenny served as CEO for five years.

In 2015, Jenny left the law firm and Cutting Edge Capital to start her own legal, coaching, and consulting practice, Jenny Kassan Consulting, a certified B Corp. She was certified as a coach by the International Association of Women in Coaching because she realized that her clients often need more than just great legal advice when raising capital.

Jenny has helped her clients raise millions of dollars, and raised several hundred thousand for her own business and for a nonprofit investment fund called the Force for Good Fund.

In 2016, Jenny was appointed to the Securities and Exchange Commission Advisory Committee on Small and Emerging Companies.

Jenny is the president of Community Ventures, a nonprofit organization dedicated to supporting community-based innovation that promotes prosperity and well-being for all. She also cofounded the Sustainable Economies Law Center, a nonprofit that provides legal information and advocacy to support sustainable economies.

Jenny is a member of the Content Advisory Panel of *Conscious Company* magazine and serves on the advisory boards of *Lioness* magazine and Investibule. She is also a fellow at Democracy Collaborative, an organization that works to create an equitable, inclusive, and sustainable economy.

Jenny lives in Fremont, California, with her politician–software developer–bird photographer husband.

For more information about Jenny's work and services, visit www.jennykassan.com.

Berrett–Koehler
Publishers

Berrett-Koehler is an independent publisher dedicated to an ambitious mission: *Connecting people and ideas to create a world that works for all.*

We believe that the solutions to the world's problems will come from all of us, working at all levels: in our organizations, in our society, and in our own lives. Our BK Business books help people make their organizations more humane, democratic, diverse, and effective (we don't think there's any contradiction there). Our BK Currents books offer pathways to creating a more just, equitable, and sustainable society. Our BK Life books help people create positive change in their lives and align their personal practices with their aspirations for a better world.

All of our books are designed to bring people seeking positive change together around the ideas that empower them to see and shape the world in a new way.

And we strive to practice what we preach. At the core of our approach is Stewardship, a deep sense of responsibility to administer the company for the benefit of all of our stakeholder groups including authors, customers, employees, investors, service providers, and the communities and environment around us. Everything we do is built around this and our other key values of quality, partnership, inclusion, and sustainability.

This is why we are both a B-Corporation and a California Benefit Corporation—a certification and a for-profit legal status that require us to adhere to the highest standards for corporate, social, and environmental performance.

We are grateful to our readers, authors, and other friends of the company who consider themselves to be part of the BK Community. We hope that you, too, will join us in our mission.

A BK Life Book

BK Life books help people clarify and align their values, aspirations, and actions. Whether you want to manage your time more effectively or uncover your true purpose, these books are designed to instigate infectious positive change that starts with you. Make your mark!

To find out more, visit **www.bkconnection.com**.

Berrett–Koehler
Publishers

Connecting people and ideas
to create a world that works for all

Dear Reader,

Thank you for picking up this book and joining our worldwide community of Berrett-Koehler readers. We share ideas that bring positive change into people's lives, organizations, and society.

To welcome you, we'd like to offer you a free e-book. You can pick from among twelve of our bestselling books by entering the promotional code **BKP92E** here: http://www.bkconnection.com/welcome.

When you claim your free e-book, we'll also send you a copy of our e-newsletter, the *BK Communiqué*. Although you're free to unsubscribe, there are many benefits to sticking around. In every issue of our newsletter you'll find

- A free e-book
- Tips from famous authors
- Discounts on spotlight titles
- Hilarious insider publishing news
- A chance to win a prize for answering a riddle

Best of all, our readers tell us, "Your newsletter is the only one I actually read." So claim your gift today, and please stay in touch!

Sincerely,

Charlotte Ashlock
Steward of the BK Website

Questions? Comments? Contact me at bkcommunity@bkpub.com.

Certified
B
Corporation
bcorporation.net